T0249336

WHAT YOU NEED TO KNOW

About the

RAPTURE

CHARLES C. RYRIE

HARVEST PROPHECY

AN IMPRINT OF HARVEST HOUSE PUBLISHERS

Unless otherwise indicated, all Scripture verses are taken from the (NASB®) New American Standard Bible®, Copyright © 1960, 1971, 1977 by The Lockman Foundation. Used by permission. All rights reserved. www.lockman.org.

Verses marked KJV are taken from the King James Version of the Bible.

Cover design by Studio Gearbox
Cover image © Javier Pardina / Stocksy
Interior design by Janelle Coury

For bulk, special sales, or ministry purchases, please call 1-800-547-8979.
Email: CustomerService@hhpbooks.com

This logo is a federally registered trademark of the Hawkins Children's LLC. Harvest House Publishers, Inc., is the exclusive licensee of this trademark.

What You Need to Know About the Rapture
Copyright © 1996 by Charles C. Ryrie
Published by Harvest House Publishers
Eugene, Oregon 97408
www.harvesthousepublishers.com

ISBN 978-0-7369-9013-4 (hardcover)
ISBN 978-0-7369-9014-1 (eBook)

Library of Congress Control Number: 2024931371

All rights reserved. No part of this publication may be reproduced, stored in a retrieval system, or transmitted in any form or by any means—electronic, mechanical, digital, photocopy, recording, or any other—except for brief quotations in printed reviews, without the prior permission of the publisher.

Printed in Colombia

24 25 26 27 28 29 30 31 32 / NI / 10 9 8 7 6 5 4 3 2

CONTENTS

Foreword by Jack Hibbs 5

1. What Are the Questions? 9

2. Are the Questions Important? 19

3. What Is the Rapture? 25

4. Two Futures? 33

5. The Vocabulary for the Second Coming . . . 41

6. What Does 2 Thessalonians 1 Really Say? . . 47

7. Where Is the Church in Revelation 4–18? . . 55

8. Where Did the Pretrib View Originate? . . . 63

9. Populating the Millennial Kingdom 71

10. The Day of the Lord 89

11. Wrath or Rapture? 107

Notes 121

FOREWORD

JACK HIBBS

From the very outset of the New Testament revelation, Jesus Christ made it clear that for His people, the church, there would come a time when, at the end of her earthly commissioning, the Lord Himself would call His followers up into the atmosphere to meet Him in the air as He clearly stated: "Let not your heart be troubled; you believe in God, believe also in Me. In My Father's house are many mansions; if it were not so, I would have told you. I go to prepare a place for you. And if I go and prepare a place for you, I will come again and receive you to Myself; that where I am, there you may be also" (John 14:1-3). This spectacular announcement that the church would one day be happily interrupted by His sudden appearing continues to be the hope and comfort of every longing heart.

Unfortunately, far too many Christians have not been taught the full counsel of God, let alone its eschatological doctrines. Yet it is Bible prophecy that stands invincible before an unbelieving world and sets the Bible apart from all religious writings. It is the perfect, unwavering, and inerrant testimony that the God of Abraham, Isaac, and Jacob dwells outside of time and speaks regarding past and future events. No one articulates this more clearly than Dr. Charles C. Ryrie.

During his incredible career, Dr. Ryrie authored more than 50 books, including *The Holy Spirit, Transformed by His Glory, So Great Salvation*, and one of my favorites, *Basic Theology: A Popular Systematic Guide to Understanding Biblical Truth*. I am reminded of Dr. Ryrie every morning when I open what I consider to be his most remarkable work, *The Ryrie Study Bible*.

Those acquainted with Dr. Ryrie knew him to be an avid student of God's Word and gifted at making the Bible's eschatological or end-times teachings easy to understand. In *What You Need to Know About the Rapture*, Dr. Ryrie draws from his voluminous writings, lectures, and studies to give a simple, concise, and biblically accurate understanding of what the Bible teaches regarding the rapture. You will learn its biblical origins, why it is consistent with the whole of Scripture, and how the rapture plays such a pivotal role in the spiritual well-being of the church in the last days. *What You Need to Know About the Rapture* is an excellent introduction to the foundations of the biblical argument for the rapture of the church.

I cannot stress enough the incredible benefits you will receive from reading this outstanding work that we would not only expect to receive from Dr. Ryrie but have consistently come to enjoy from him over decades as a faithful servant of God.

Awaiting His return,
Jack Hibbs, pastor
Calvary Chapel Chino Hills and Real Life Network

1

WHAT ARE
THE QUESTIONS?

Can anyone predict the future?

Many people hope someone can, and some try. Millions read the horoscope columns every day, and the money spent on phone calls to psychics speaks for itself. Clearly, people long to know what the future holds for them, for their families, and for the world itself.

World events are a constant cause of worry for many people, and for good reasons. In recent years, we have seen rioting, violent attacks, shooting sprees, and rampant crime. Piled onto these senseless, lawless acts are economic and health crises that have many people worried. Corporations have reduced their work forces without much notice. And there are unstable conditions in countries all around the world.

There are many global political uncertainties that disturb people. Tensions are rising in Europe, Asia, South America, and Africa. The ongoing conflicts in the Middle East cause deep concern. People are wondering about the advancements being made toward the making of nuclear weapons. Does North Korea have the bomb? Does Iran? Our world is never free of wars, and there is the continual threat that new wars could break out. Will there ever be widespread peace? And so it goes. No wonder ordinary people are concerned about the world, its future, and their place in it.

But who has the answers? Can anyone make truly accurate predictions? Politicians? Fortune tellers? Astrologers? Futurologists? Columnists? Preachers? Only the Bible has the answers. Only the Bible offers true and accurate prophecies. It reveals that not until Jesus Christ returns to the earth will the world experience peace and safety, and that will happen under His government. The Bible also reveals that before Jesus returns, times will become worse and worse—indeed, worse than ever before. And then the time of the dreadful Tribulation period will come.

The great Tribulation worries many believers. Will they have to go through the Tribulation? Some say yes. These believe that the "catching away" of the church will not occur until the end of the Tribulation. Others say no. They believe Christians will be raptured before the Tribulation begins. This book examines these two different time scenarios. But before we consider the *time* of the rapture, we need to survey the different millennial viewpoints.

The Millennial Question

The millennial question asks what kind of Millennium there will be. That there will be some kind of Millennium is clearly taught in Revelation 20:1-6. But what kind of Millennium that will be is and has been strongly debated through the years. Early Christians expected Jesus Christ's speedy return to establish an actual kingdom on this earth, over which He would reign for 1,000 years. This premillennial view of the return of Christ was taught by almost all the church fathers of the first two centuries.

When Christ did not return as soon as some people thought He would, the church's concept of the Millennium changed to a nonliteral one called "amillennialism." Augustine (354–430) taught people to look for a Millennium that would be wholly spiritual in character during the Christian dispensation. During the Middle Ages and the Reformation periods, the idea of an actual kingdom was not taught by mainline groups, some of whom considered such teaching heretical. In the seventeenth century, a new millennial teaching, postmillennialism, appeared. It affirmed that before the return of Christ there would be a worldwide experience of peace and righteousness due to the efforts of the church.

THREE VIEWS OF CHRIST'S RETURN

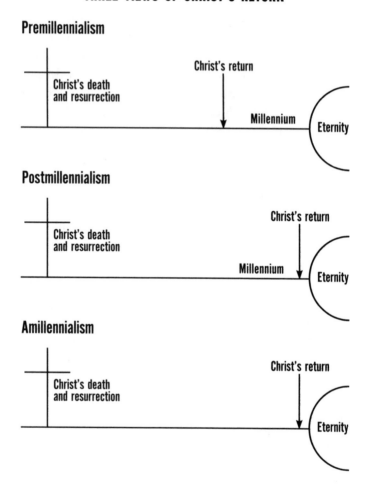

Premillennialism

Christ's death
and resurrection

Christ's return

Millennium

Eternity

Postmillennialism

Christ's death
and resurrection

Christ's return

Millennium

Eternity

Amillennialism

Christ's death
and resurrection

Christ's return

Eternity

Since then, there has been a revival of premillennialism, a continuation of amillennialism, and most recently, a resurgence of postmillennialism.

These viewpoints—pre-, post-, and amillennialism—concern the relation of the coming of Jesus Christ to the Millennium, His 1,000-year reign.

The Rapture Question

In the nineteenth century, teachings about the rapture of the church began to be widely disseminated. This raised such questions as whether the second coming of Christ involves several stages, the relation of those stages to the Tribulation period, and the distinctiveness of the church from Israel in God's program. Thus, one of the prominent eschatological questions of this century is the question of the timing of the rapture and its ramifications for the total picture of the future.

For the *amillennialist*, the single event of Christ's second coming is followed by a general resurrection, judgment, and eternity. For the *postmillennialist*, there is also no distinct rapture; a second coming after the Millennium has already been brought about by the church, and eternity follows. *Premillennialists* agree that the rapture and second coming are distinguishable, although they do not agree as to how much time separates them.

Pretrib and Posttrib

The principal disagreement today lies between pre-tribulationists and posttribulationists, both of which are premillennial. *Pretribulationists* teach that Christ's coming for His church—the rapture—will occur before the Tribulation (the entire seventieth "week" of Daniel) begins. *Posttribulationists* teach that the rapture and the second coming are facets of a single event occurring at the conclusion of the Tribulation. Both agree that the second coming of Christ will be followed by the Millennium on earth. Those are the principal views we will discuss in this book.

Midtrib and Partial Rapture

There are at least two other views about the rapture's timing. One is the midtribulation view. It teaches, as its name reveals, that the church will be taken to heaven (raptured) in the middle of the Tribulation period. Since the Tribulation will last seven years, this means that the church will be on earth for the first three-and-one-half of those years.

Like pretribulationists, midtribulationists teach that the rapture and the second coming are separated by a period of time: seven years for the pretribulationists and three-and-one-half for midtribulationists. Both teach that the church will be delivered from the wrath of the Tribulation period. Other aspects of the midtrib view include

PREMILLENNIAL RAPTURE TIMING VIEWS

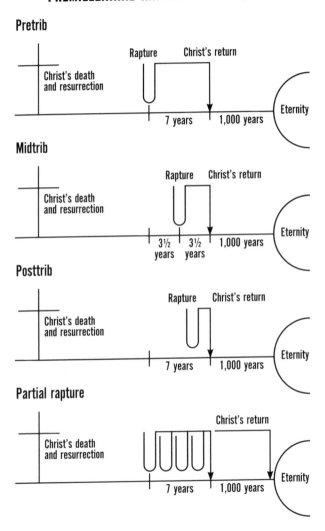

Pretrib

Christ's death and resurrection

Rapture

Christ's return

7 years | 1,000 years

Eternity

Midtrib

Christ's death and resurrection

Rapture

Christ's return

3½ years | 3½ years | 1,000 years

Eternity

Posttrib

Christ's death and resurrection

Rapture

Christ's return

7 years | 1,000 years

Eternity

Partial rapture

Christ's death and resurrection

Christ's return

7 years | 1,000 years

Eternity

identifying the last trumpet of 1 Corinthians 15:52 with the seventh trumpet of Revelation 11:15, and interpreting the two witnesses of Revelation 11 as symbolic of the larger group of raptured people at the middle of the Tribulation. Most of the arguments that support the midtrib view argue against the posttrib view.

Whereas pre-, mid-, and posttrib views focus on the time of the rapture, the partial rapture view focuses on the people to be raptured. It teaches that only those believers who are "watching" and "waiting" for the Lord's return will be worthy to escape the Tribulation by being raptured.

Actually, the partial rapture view teaches that there will be several raptures. Like pretribulationists, partial rapture proponents teach that one rapture will occur at the beginning of the Tribulation to take away spiritually mature saints. Then at various times during the seven years of Tribulation, other raptures will remove saints who were unprepared at the beginning of the Tribulation but who have shown themselves worthy in the meantime. There is even to be a rapture at the close of the Millennium.

Generally speaking, the partial rapture teaching understands verses like Luke 21:34-36 and Revelation 3:10 as distinguishing two kinds of saints: those who will be raptured and those who will be left in the trial.

Diagrammed, the four answers given to the question by premillennialists appear on page 15.

To sum up, this chapter has shown us that the church

has questions about the Millennium and the rapture. Throughout the following pages, we will primarily discuss the rapture and its relation to the Tribulation period. We won't be discussing very much about millennial views, except as premillennialism relates to pre- and posttribulationists. But before we get to that, we need to ask: "Are such questions even that important?"

2

ARE THE QUESTIONS
IMPORTANT?

oes it really make any difference when the Lord will come? Is it not His coming itself that is important, rather than when?

Are all biblical doctrines of equal importance? In one sense, yes; in another, no. That God has chosen to reveal something makes it important—even a genealogy. Therefore, everything in the Bible is of equal importance from the perspective of God's revelation.

On the other hand, one can certainly be saved without knowing much about God's revelation in the Bible.

Truths about salvation and about the accuracy and authority of the Bible would obviously stand at the top of any list of important doctrines. Yet this is not to say that biblical teachings about the future or about demons or about the church are unimportant. But by comparison to how a person is saved, such doctrines are not as important as the gospel is.

End-Time Affair

How important is eschatology? Even the message of salvation includes something about eternal life, something about future judgment, and something about the Judge who is going to intervene in the affairs of mankind (Acts 17:31). Yet the chief question of this book, the timing of the rapture, does not have to be settled or even understood in order for people to be saved.

There are several reasons, however, that this is an important question.

Prophecy

Prophecy is important to biblical revelation. It is said that one-fourth of the Bible was prophecy when it was written (of course, many of those prophecies have been fulfilled), and that one out of every five verses in Paul's writings concerns prophecy. Passages concerning the rapture form an important part of this prophetic material concerning eschatology. Some instruction concerning the rapture comes from Paul's teachings (1 Corinthians 15:51-58; 1 Thessalonians 4:13–5:11), and some from the teachings of Christ (John 14:1-3; Revelation 3:10).

Furthermore, the Lord gave a promise to the disciples and to us concerning the teaching ministry of the Holy Spirit in this dispensation. He promised that the Spirit would "disclose to you what is to come" (John 16:13). "Things that are to come" seems to be a specific area of truth within the broader promise that the Spirit "will guide you into all the truth." In other words, special attention to prophecy is promised. Some people believe that those coming things do not refer to end-time events but to the revelation concerning the Christian church period (which was future when Christ spoke). Even if that interpretation is correct, "things that are to come" cannot exclude the events at the end of the church period, so the phrase still involves prophetic truths, including those about the rapture.

The Lord, then, expects us to understand prophecy, including prophecies about the rapture. Clearly, that doctrine cannot be ignored if we enter fully into the fulfillment of Christ's promise. (See 1 Thessalonians 5:6; Titus 2:13.)

Imminency

The question of the rapture's timing is related to the concept of imminency, which means "impending, hanging over one's head, ready to take place." An imminent event is one that is always ready to take place. Pretribs recognize that something *may* happen before an imminent event occurs, but they do not insist that anything *must* take place before it happens; otherwise, it would not be imminent. Posttribs apply imminency "to an event that is *near* and cannot at *this* point [in time] be accurately dated but that will *not* occur until some necessary preliminary events transpire."[1]

However, surely some believers living on earth during the Tribulation could "accurately date" the time of the posttrib rapture simply by determining how much time is left in the seven years. Therefore, even by the posttrib's definition of imminency, it is difficult to see how a posttrib rapture could be imminent. In the pretrib concept, no events have to take place before the rapture can occur; therefore, the rapture is imminent and has been for centuries. Further, pretribs argue that if the church is on earth during the Tribulation and will not be raptured until the end of it, then the rapture cannot be "ready to take place" until those events predicted to occur during the Tribulation first happen. Only then (that is, toward the very end of the Tribulation) would the rapture be imminent. The necessity of something having to take place before the rapture occurs weakens the concept of imminency.[2]

When I first began to teach, I did not meet many people who had clear posttrib convictions. That was partly due to the fact that I moved mostly in pretrib circles. But it was also because the posttrib view was not popular. In the several decades since, some Christians have changed from a pretrib to a posttrib position. More literature has been published. Doctrine today is not considered to be as important as experience. Cooperation among evangelicals, with a view to appealing to the largest possible audience, often precludes proclaiming eschatological distinctions. The spirit of our times looks down on dogmatism, even if it is truth.

I gladly respect different positions, especially when they are held intelligently. One of the greatest assets of Christianity in the United States has been the freedom to hold different positions and to establish churches and schools that promote them. Our differences over the rapture question need not be detrimental to the cause of Christ. We should want to study the question not to divide the church, but because it is part of God's revelation, because it comes under the umbrella of Christ's promise in John 16:13, and because it shapes our concept of imminency.

The Whole Plan

But there is one additional reason. The question is important in order to proclaim the whole plan of God accurately. I detect today a spirit of eschatological agnosticism, which is not healthy for the church. Some are saying that we cannot know (agnosticism) the answers to these minor eschatological questions, so we should simply ignore them. The church will not lose much, we are assured.

But if we lose any of God's revelation, we lose something important. We need to make up our minds about eschatological truths so that we can proclaim all of God's truth. The rapture is a vital part of eschatology. It is a question worth studying, a truth worth proclaiming.

Suffering

Finally, notice that the reasons that make this an important question do not include a desire to avoid suffering if that be God's will for us.

Pretribulationists do not hold their view as an escape mechanism. Our Lord warned that believers in every generation would suffer tribulation in this world (John 16:33). Paul said that it is normal for Christians to live under a sentence of death (Romans 8:36). The rapture question is not about Christian tribulation in general; it is about the Christian's relation to the yet-future period of tribulation.

If Christ's coming should be pretribulational, then we will praise Him because we missed that terrible time. If it is posttribulational, then we will gladly suffer for His sake. Either way, we still have the blessed hope of His coming.

3

WHAT IS THE RAPTURE?

The modern concept of *rapture* has little or nothing to do with an eschatological event. But the word is used properly of that event.

Rapture is a state or experience of being carried away. We are enraptured by the beauty of a sunset. We say that it is sheer rapture to hear a certain piece of music. When we say such things, we mean we are carried away by the experience.

The English word comes from a Latin word, *rapio,* which means "to seize or be carried away in one's spirit," or the actual removal from one place to another. In other words, it means to be carried away either in spirit or body. Thus the rapture of the church means the removal of the church from earth to heaven.

But is this a biblical term? Yes. The Greek word from which we take this term *rapture* appears in 1 Thessalonians 4:17 and is translated "caught up." The Latin translation of this verse uses the word *rapturo,* from which we derive our English word *rapture.* So it is a biblical term that has come to us through the Latin translation of 1 Thessalonians 4:17.

The original Greek word in that verse is *harpazo.* Like the Latin word, it also means to snatch or take away, and it occurs 13 times in the New Testament. It describes how the Spirit caught up Philip near Gaza and brought him to Caesarea (Acts 8:39). Paul used it to describe his experience of being caught up to the third heaven, whether in or out of his body (2 Corinthians 12:2-4). Thus there can be no doubt that it is describing an actual removal of people from earth to heaven when it is used in 1 Thessalonians 4:17 of the rapture of the church.

Five Aspects of the Rapture

What will this event be like? Paul answers this in detail in 1 Thessalonians 4:13-18 by describing five aspects of the rapture.

Jesus' Return

There will be a *return* of Christ (1 Thessalonians 4:16). The Lord Himself will come for His people, accompanied by all the grandeur His presence deserves. There will be a shout, a command such as an officer gives to his troops. The text does not say whether the Lord or an archangel will shout, though the voice of an archangel will be heard. Michael is the only archangel so named in the Bible (Jude 9), but it is possible that there are other archangels (see Daniel 10:13, and notice that Paul wrote "*an* archangel," not "*the* archangel," in the original language of 1 Thessalonians 4:16). The trumpet of God will summon the dead in Christ to their resurrection, and at the same time, it will be a warning to those who have rejected Christ that it is now too late to participate in the rapture. Clearly, the rapture will not be a silent event.

Resurrection

There will be a *resurrection* (1 Thessalonians 4:16). At this point in history, only the dead in Christ will be raised (that is, only Christians). Although there have been many believers since Adam, no believer was placed "in Christ" until the day of Pentecost, when the baptism of the Holy Spirit first occurred (Acts 2). So those raised at the rapture include all believers from the day of Pentecost until the rapture.

Priority will be given to the dead, who will be raised just before the living are changed. And yet both groups will experience their respective changes "in a moment, in the twinkling of an eye" (1 Corinthians 15:52). The entire procedure will be instantaneous, not gradual. The Greek word for "moment" comes from the word *atom*. When the atom was discovered, it was thought to be indivisible, so it was named "atom." Even though subsequently the atom was split, the word still means "indivisible." The rapture will occur in an indivisible instant of time, like the twinkling of the eye.

Rapture

There will be a *rapture* (1 Thessalonians 4:17). Living believers will be caught up into the Lord's presence without experiencing physical death. In the past, two others went to heaven without dying: Enoch and Elijah. That is why Paul called this translation from life on earth to life in heaven, without dying, a mystery (1 Corinthians 15:51). Paul's use of the word *mystery* is like waving a flag to let us know that he is about to tell us something that had not been revealed before. Resurrection was not unknown, for the Old Testament spoke of the resurrection of the dead (Job 19:25; Isaiah 26:19; Daniel 12:2). So did Christ (John 5:26-29). But nowhere had God revealed that a large group of people would not have to die, but would go directly from this life into God's presence. While Enoch's and Elijah's experiences illustrated the rapture, they did not promise that experience to anyone.

In 1 Corinthians 15:51-54, Paul tells us how the rapture will happen. The bodies of those who have died before the

Lord comes will have experienced corruption; therefore, they will need to put on incorruption at this time of resurrection. But the bodies of living believers will not have experienced the corruption of death; they will be mortal. So they will put on immortality by some unexplained process of replacing bodies subject to death (mortal) with bodies that will never die (immortal).

Strictly speaking, the word *rapture* relates only to the experience of living believers who are caught up into the Lord's presence. However, theologically speaking, *rapture* is used for this entire event, including the resurrection of believers who have died as well as the translation of believers who are alive.

Reunion

There will be a *reunion* (1 Thessalonians 4:17), first with loved ones, and second, with the Lord. In that instant of resurrection and translation, there will be countless reunions with loved ones. But the excitement of those reunions will pale in the light of what it will mean to see the Lord.

Where will He take us then? To the heavenly abodes He is now preparing for His own (John 14:1-3). According to the pretrib view, the church will be judged and rewarded in heaven while the seven years of Tribulation are being experienced on earth; then Christ and His church will return in great glory to the earth at the end of the Tribulation to execute other judgments and to establish His millennial kingdom.

Reassurance

There is *reassurance* from this doctrine (1 Thessalonians 4:18). "Therefore," Paul wrote, "comfort one another with these words." The word *comfort* also means "encourage." The doctrine of the rapture comforts all who have lost loved ones. Believers do not have to sorrow as those who have no eternal hope. The truth of the rapture encourages us with a certain knowledge and a firm hope about the future. Loved ones will be raised, and living ones will be changed when the Lord comes.

These comforting and encouraging truths are valid whether one holds to the pre-, mid-, or posttribulation view. But the partial rapture concept diminishes the comforting and encouraging aspects of this doctrine. In that view there are several raptures, and all of them are rewards for overcomers. Thus the Tribulation becomes a kind of purgatory, and the raptures become times of release from that purgatory.

Furthermore, Paul's descriptions of the rapture in both 1 Corinthians 15 and 1 Thessalonians 4 disagree with the partial rapture view. Paul said that it would be in a single moment, not throughout seven or more years, that "we shall all be changed," and not just the spiritual ones (1 Corinthians 15:51). And he wrote those reassuring words to the Corinthians, many of whom could hardly be called overcomers as defined by partial rapturists!

4

TWO FUTURES?

Before examining specific passages that pre- and posttribulationists use to support their positions, it will be helpful to sketch the broad picture each view paints of the future.

Obviously, not all adherents to either view agree on all the details. Also, pretribulationists have projected a much more detailed picture of the future than have posttribulationists, who generally have concentrated on countering pretribulation arguments rather than on putting together a chronology of the future.

The Pretrib Future

The pretrib view sees the rapture as the next event on God's program. It will occur before the Tribulation begins, the actual beginning being signaled by the signing of the pact between Israel and the leader of the revived Roman Empire, ruled by the man of sin. This event actually begins the seventieth week of Daniel (9:25-27), the seven-year Tribulation period, during which the church will be absent from the earth in fulfillment of the promise of Revelation 3:10. The Tribulation also begins the Day of the Lord, which totally includes that period and the judgments at the second coming of Christ and the Millennium. At the beginning of the seven years, 144,000 Jews will be sealed, saved, and protected in order to serve God during that time. Also, the worldwide church will gain great political power before being destroyed at the middle of the Tribulation. The seal judgments of Revelation 6 (or at least most of them) will be poured out on the earth as part of the wrath during the first half of the Tribulation.

At the midpoint, the two witnesses of Revelation 11 will be killed and raised. The ecumenical church will be overthrown. Satan will be cast out of heaven to begin even more intense persecution of the Jewish people (Revelation 12:9, 13). The man of sin will break his pact with Israel and seek to extend his dominion both politically and religiously. He will demand that the world worship him.

In the latter half of the Tribulation, other horrible judgments will fall on the earth (Revelation 8–9; 16). Egypt will fall, the great alliance to the north of Israel will attack, armies from the east will move into Israel, and the campaign of Armageddon will be ended by the return of Christ.

PRETRIB VIEW

1. Rapture occurs before the Tribulation

2. Church experiences Revelation 3:10 before the Tribulation

3. Day of the Lord begins with the Tribulation

4. 1 Thessalonians 5:2-3 occurs at beginning of the Tribulation

5. 144,000 redeemed at start of the Tribulation

6. Rapture and second coming separated by seven years

7. Living Israelites judged at second coming

8. Living Gentiles judged at second coming

9. Parents of millennial population come from survivors of judgments on living Jews and Gentiles

10. Believers of church age judged in heaven between rapture and second coming

Then judgments will fall on Jewish people who have survived the Tribulation (Ezekiel 20:33-44) and on Gentile survivors (Matthew 25:31-46). People who are acquitted in those judgments will be those who accepted Christ, and they will then enter the millennial kingdom in unresurrected earthly bodies to become the parents of the millennial population.

Christ will then set up His kingdom and reign on this earth for 1,000 years. At the conclusion, Satan will be let loose to lead one final unsuccessful revolution. All unbelievers of all time will be raised to appear at the judgment of the great white throne and then to be cast into the lake of fire forever.

The Posttrib Future

The posttrib view also sees the seventieth week of Daniel as yet future. But in this view, the church will not be raptured before the seventieth week begins. Rather, the church will be on the earth during the entire seven-year Tribulation period. There will be no rapture to signal the imminent signing of a pact between the man of sin and Israel. Instead, that agreement will be signed, and the Tribulation will begin, in the normal ongoing course of political affairs in the world. The seal, trumpet, and bowl judgments will occur during that time (concurrently rather than sequentially). Those will not be the wrath of God, however, but the wrath of Satan and man. The wrath of God will not be poured out until the very end of the Tribulation. The 144,000 will be protected by God from dying throughout the period, but they will not be saved until the second coming. Some posttribulationists consider the 144,000 to be a symbolic representation of the church rather than a specific number of Jewish people.

POSTTRIB VIEW

1. Rapture occurs after the Tribulation

2. Church experiences Revelation 3:10 at end of Tribulation

3. Day of the Lord begins at close of Tribulation

4. 1 Thessalonians 5:2-3 occurs near end of Tribulation

5. 144,000 redeemed at conclusion of Tribulation

6. Rapture and second coming are a single event

7. No such judgment of living Israelites at second coming

8. Living Gentiles judged after Millennium

9. Parents of millennial population come from 144,000 Jews

10. Believers of church age judged after second coming or at conclusion of Millennium

At the end of the Tribulation, the Day of the Lord will begin, preceded by a peaceful lull in the horrible events that will have been going on (to fulfill 1 Thessalonians 5:2-3). Then the church will experience the fulfillment of Revelation 3:10 and emerge from within the Tribulation period just at its end, missing the battle of Armageddon.

Yet the rapture will be a single event with the second coming, with the church meeting the Lord in the air and then immediately turning around to descend to the earth.

When the Lord returns, there will be no formal judgment of Tribulation survivors. The 144,000 will be saved at that point (assuming the view that they are indeed Jewish people and not representative of the church) and will enter the Millennium in unresurrected bodies. The judgment of the living Gentiles of Matthew 25:31-46 will not occur until the end of the Millennium, at the same time as the judgment of unbelievers at the great white throne.

Where the Two Views Agree

Notice the points of agreement between these two views.

1. The seventieth week of Daniel is yet future and will begin with the signing of a treaty between Israel and the man of sin.

2. The earth will literally experience the judgments described in the book of Revelation (though some posttribulationists tend to deliteralize some of them).

3. The second coming will usher in the millennial kingdom of Christ.

4. The great white throne judgment of unbelievers
   will take place after the Millennium.

So we have points of agreement and disagreement in
the two chronologies. Now we are ready to examine the
pros and cons of the Scriptures on which they are based.

5

THE VOCABULARY FOR
THE SECOND COMING

D o the words used for the second coming in the New Testament indicate that it will be a single event (posttrib view), or do they describe two events separated by seven years (pretrib view)?

Posttribulationists claim, "The parousia, the apokalypse, and the epiphany appear to be a single event. Any division of Christ's coming into two parts is an unproven inference."[1]

To put their argument another way: Since New Testament writers use several words to describe the second coming, if the rapture and return are separate events, why did they not reserve one word for the rapture and another for the return, instead of apparently using the words interchangeably?[2]

Parousia

Parousia, meaning "coming," "arrival," or "presence," is used in relation to the rapture in 1 Thessalonians 4:15. It also describes the second coming of Christ in Matthew 24:27. Two different conclusions are possible from this usage: 1) *Parousia* describes the same, single event, meaning that the rapture and the second coming are a single event at the end of the Tribulation, or 2) *parousia* describes two separate events, both characterized by the presence of the Lord, but events that will not happen at the same time. Either conclusion is valid.

Here is an illustration. Suppose proud grandparents should say to their friends, "We are looking forward to enjoying the presence [*parousia*] of our grandchildren next week." Then later in the conversation, they add, "Yes, we expect our grandchildren to be present at our golden wedding celebration." If you heard those statements, you could draw either of two conclusions: 1) The grandchildren are coming next week for the golden wedding anniversary. In other words, the grandparents were speaking of the coming and the anniversary as a single event occurring at the same time. 2) The grandchildren will be making two trips to see their grandparents—one next week (as part of their vacation, say), and another later to help celebrate the golden wedding anniversary.

Likewise, since the Lord's presence (*parousia*) will characterize both the rapture and the second coming, the word itself does not indicate whether these are a single event or separate events. In other words, the vocabulary used does not necessarily prove either pre- or posttrib views.

Apokalupsis

A second word used for the Lord's coming is *apoka-lupsis,* meaning "revelation." It occurs in rapture passages like 1 Corinthians 1:7 and 1 Peter 1:7; 4:13 because, when Christ comes for the church, He will reveal Himself to her. At His coming, the church will see Him as He is. The word also appears in passages that describe His coming to the earth at the close of the Tribulation (2 Thessalonians 1:7) because that event also will reveal Christ to the world.

Two conclusions are possible: 1) The rapture and the second coming are the same single event. Since both are called a revelation of Christ, they must occur at the same time and be part of the same event at the end of the Tribulation. 2) Both the rapture and the second coming will reveal Christ, but not at the same time or under the same circumstances. Therefore, the rapture and the second coming can be separated, as the pretrib view teaches.

The first conclusion uses the word *revelation* as a *cataloging* word—that is, in all the passages where the word is used, it catalogs whatever event is referred to as the same, single event. The second conclusion sees the word *revelation* as a *characterizing* word—that is, it is used to characterize different events in the same way, as a revelation.

It becomes more obvious, then, that the vocabulary used in the New Testament does not seem to prove either the pre- or posttrib view. But let's pursue the matter further.

Epiphaneia

The third principal word used for the second coming is *epiphaneia*, meaning "manifestation." At the second coming, Christ will destroy Antichrist by the sheer manifestation of His coming (2 Thessalonians 2:8). The word is also used in reference to the hope of the believer when he will see the Lord (2 Timothy 4:8; Titus 2:13). Are we to conclude that the word is *cataloging* those references to refer them to the same single event? Or can we conclude that it is *characterizing* two different events, both involving a manifestation of Christ but not occurring at the same time? The answer is either, but not both!

Clearly, then, the vocabulary does not prove either a pre- or posttrib view of the rapture. Why, then, does this vocabulary continue to be used? Simply because posttribulationists continue to believe that it is a valid support for their view, even claiming that it "substantiates" their view.[3]

But the posttribulationists' underlying assumption in continuing to use this argument is that these words *catalog* rather than *characterize*. To be sure, the vocabulary might do that; but to be equally sure, it might not.

Take the word *motor*. A washing machine has a motor.

A furnace fan has a motor. Automobiles have a motor. Is the term *motor* a characterizing feature of these diverse products? Or is it a means of cataloging them, which would force us to conclude that everything that has a motor is the same thing? The answer is obvious.

Do presence, revelation, and manifestation characterize different events or catalog the same event? The pretribulationist says the former; the posttribulationist concludes the latter.

6

WHAT DOES 2 THESSALONIANS 1 REALLY SAY?

Some posttribulationists find an important argument for their position in 2 Thessalonians 1:5-10:

> This is a plain indication of God's righteous judgment so that you may be considered worthy of the kingdom of God, for which indeed you are suffering. For after all it is only just for God to repay with affliction those who afflict you, and to give relief to you who are afflicted and to us as well when the Lord Jesus shall be revealed from heaven with His mighty angels in flaming fire, dealing out retribution to those who do not know God and to those who do not obey the gospel of our Lord Jesus. And

these will pay the penalty of eternal destruction, away from the presence of the Lord and
from the glory of His power, when He comes
to be glorified in His saints on that day, and to
be marveled at among all who have believed—
for our testimony to you was believed.

Posttribulationists understand the passage to say that
"Paul places the release of Christians from persecution at
the posttribulational return of Christ to judge unbelievers, whereas according to pretribulationism this release will
occur seven years earlier."[1] In other words, since release
comes at the second coming and release is connected with
the rapture, the rapture must happen at the same time as
the second coming. This is different from what the pretrib
view says.

Conflicting Views

Let's see why this posttrib position on 2 Thessalonians 1
conflicts with the pretrib view. The conflict affects chiefly
three areas of the passage: the group of people meant, the
time of the release, and the apostle's subject.

The People

If we ask ourselves what group of people will experience this release from the posttrib position, the answer is
only those Christians who survive the Tribulation and are

alive at the (posttrib) rapture. Thus, the passage addresses only the release of Christians living at the conclusion of the Tribulation.

If that is true, why does Paul seemingly ignore the Thessalonians, who had suffered persecution and who had already died? Death was the means of release for them. Indeed, why does he not mention that avenue of release, which some of those to whom he was writing might yet experience? To be sure, the rapture of the living will bring release from persecution, but only a relatively small percentage of believers will ever experience that means of release, since most will have died prior to the rapture. If release is Paul's chief concern here, and if that release will come at the posttrib rapture, then Paul is offering that hope of release to a very small group of believers.

The Timing

From the posttrib slant, we must also conclude that the release for Christians is timed with the flaming judgment on unbelievers. It is not described in terms of meeting the Lord and forever being with Him, or in terms of a resurrection for those who have died, as other rapture passages describe it. Obviously if one's enemies are punished, then there will be a release from their persecution. But the point is this: Where is the rapture described at all in this passage? It is the judgmental aspect of the second coming that is given the prominence. According to posttribulationism, although the rapture is the initial part of the second coming, that initial part *is entirely absent* from this discussion.

If Paul so clearly believed in a posttrib rapture, then why did he not at least mention that rapture in passing, since it is the moment of rapture that brings release, not the following judgment on God's enemies? Christians who live through the tribulation (if the posttrib view is correct) will be released from persecution the instant they are raptured, *whether or not* Christ judges their enemies at that same time.

Notice some of the words in this passage that emphasize God judging His enemies: "righteous judgment" (verse 5), "just" (verse 6), "repay" (verse 6), "affliction" (verse 6), "flaming fire" (verse 7), and "retribution" (verse 8). This vocabulary is strangely absent from the rapture passages of John 14:1-3, 1 Corinthians 15:51-58, and 1 Thessalonians 4:13-18. The rapture can be found in this 2 Thessalonians passage only if one's eschatological scheme superimposes it there. Exegesis does not produce the rapture from this passage.

The Subject

The posttrib view has the passage jumbled because it gets the apostle's subject wrong. The posttrib view sees the subject as release for Christians from persecution.

The subject, however, is not release but *vindication*. Paul does not focus on when or how the persecuted Thessalonians will be relieved of persecution; rather, he assures them that God will judge His enemies and thereby vindicate those who have suffered.

One of the most spectacular displays of God's judgment will occur at the second coming of Christ, when the armies of the world, arrayed at Armageddon, are defeated by Him and all living people will have to appear before Him (Ezekiel 20:33-44; Matthew 25:31-46). It is on those people living at that time that vengeance will fall. Dead rejecters of Christ will not be judged until after the Millennium at the great white throne. Looking back, we know that none of the unsaved who actually persecuted the Thessalonians will be judged at the second coming, but at the great white throne.

Since vindication is the subject, that explains why Paul did not mention the rapture in this passage. The rapture is not a time of God's vindication. It is a time of release, of hope, of meeting the Lord. Some Thessalonians had found release through death even before Paul wrote. Eventually all of them found it that way. Since the first century, many persecuted Christians have found the same release through death. Some will find it at the pretrib rapture. But only those believers living at the end of the Tribulation will find it then—not because a rapture takes place then, but because they successfully pass the judgments and see their enemies condemned.

But if vindication at the second coming falls on a relatively small group of Christ's enemies (think, by comparison, of the many who have opposed Him through the centuries), why should this particular time of vindication be given such prominence? Simply because the end of the Tribulation will bring to a climax the long rebellion of mankind, a rebellion that will be halted by the personal intervention of the Lord. Not all of the Lord's enemies will be judged then, but those who are the epitome of rebellion will be. Awful as the persecution of the Thessalonians may have been, as horrible as subsequent persecutions of believers may have been, they do not compare with that which will occur during the Tribulation period.

Perhaps an analogy will be helpful. Antichrists were present in the first century (1 John 2:18), and antichrists have come and gone throughout the centuries. But one great Antichrist is yet to appear, and he will be the epitome of opposition to God. Other antichrists are now in Hades awaiting the judgment at the end of the Millennium that will cast them into the lake of fire forever. But the coming great Antichrist will be judged at the second coming; and when he is, God will be vindicated over all antichrists, though their particular judgment will occur much later.

All persecutors of believers will also be judged later. The judgment of those who are alive at the second coming will vindicate God's righteousness with respect to them and to all persecutors who died before them.

If death or the rapture brings release from personal persecution, why should believers be concerned with this future vindication? Because the case against persecutors cannot be closed until Christ is vindicated and righteousness prevails. Persecution may cease when death occurs, but the case against the persecutors will not be closed until they are judged. And believers are concerned not only about relief but about vindication.

A biblical example of this is seen in the Tribulation martyrs in heaven, before the end of the Tribulation, who cry out to God for vindication (Revelation 6:9-11). "When will You settle the score against those who killed us?" they ask. Of course, they have already obtained release through physical death and are in heaven; yet they are still concerned about vindication. And the Lord replies that they will have to wait a little longer for that vindication until others are also martyred on earth.

The conclusion of the matter is that in 1 Thessalonians 1:10 and 5:9, Paul extended the hope and assurance of escape from wrath by means of a pretrib rapture. In 2 Thessalonians 1, he assured his readers that the enemies of the Lord will be judged.

Second Thessalonians 1 does not teach that release from persecution will necessarily occur at the same time as the second coming. It does not picture the rapture at all; it focuses on the judgment of the wicked and the vindication of Christ that will occur at the second coming. That vindication gives assurance to saints of all ages that righteousness will prevail.

7

WHERE IS THE CHURCH IN REVELATION 4–18?

Pretribulationists consider it a significant support to their view that the church is not mentioned even once by name in Revelation 4–18, chapters that describe the Tribulation on earth. By contrast, the word *church* occurs 19 times in chapters 1, 2, and 3, and once in chapter 22. And the phrase "wife of the Lamb" appears once in chapter 21. Yet in chapters 4–18 there is a silence about the church, which indicates to pretribulationists that the church will not be present on the earth during the Tribulation years.

Posttribulationists disagree with this for three reasons: 1) If the church is supposed to be in heaven during the events recorded in chapters 4–18, why is it not mentioned as being there? 2) The occurrence of the word *saints* in 13:7,

10; 16:6; 17:6; and 18:24 shows that the church is indeed on the earth during the Tribulation. 3) Other descriptions of believers in the Tribulation aptly apply to church-age believers; therefore, Tribulation believers will be the last generation of church-age believers, and that last generation will go through the Tribulation.

True Identities

The Church in Heaven

Pretribulationists are able to answer the first of these posttrib responses along either or both of these two lines.

1. Most identify the 24 elders as representing the church, and since they are seen in heaven in Revelation 4:4 and 5:8-10, the church is mentioned as in heaven. Some think this argument is no good because the critical text of 5:9-10 has the elders singing about redemption in the third person, as if redemption were not their own experience (thus they could not represent the church, which has been redeemed). But this is a weak argument; after all, Moses sang of redemption in the third person right after he experienced it (Exodus 15:13, 16-17).

2. Pretribulationists also point out that Hebrew marriage customs argue for the church's being

in heaven before the coming of Christ at the end of the Tribulation. Jewish marriages included a number of steps: first, betrothal (which involved the prospective groom's traveling from his father's house to the home of the prospective bride, paying the purchase price, and thus establishing the marriage covenant); second, the groom's returning to his father's house (which meant remaining separate from his bride for 12 months, during which time he prepared the living accommodations for his wife in his father's house); third, the groom's coming for his bride at a time not known exactly to her; fourth, his return with her to the groom's father's house to consummate the marriage and to celebrate the wedding feast for the next seven days (during which the bride remained closeted in her bridal chamber).

In Revelation 19:7-9, the wedding feast is announced, which, if the analogy of the Hebrew marriage customs means anything, assumes that the wedding has previously taken place in the father's house. Today, the church is described as a virgin waiting for her bridegroom's coming (2 Corinthians 11:2). In Revelation 21:9, she is designated as the wife of the Lamb, indicating that previously, she was taken to the groom's father's house. Pretribulationists say that this requires an interval of time between the rapture and the second coming. Granted, it does not say seven years' time, but it certainly argues against the posttrib view, which has no time between the rapture and second coming.

The Word Saints

The appearance of the word *saints* in chapters 4–18 does not prove anything until you know what saints they are. There were saints (godly ones) in the Old Testament (Psalm 85:8); there are saints today (1 Corinthians 1:2); there will be saints during the Tribulation years (Revelation 13:7). The question is, Are the saints of this church age distinct from saints of the Tribulation period (pretrib) or not (posttrib)? The uses of the word do not answer the question.

Other Descriptive Phrases

Such phrases include "die in the Lord" (Revelation 14:13; compare "dead in Christ" in 1 Thessalonians 4:16-18) and "those who keep the commandments of God" (Revelation 12:17; 14:12; compare Revelation 1:9). To use these similarities to prove that the church will be present in the Tribulation requires that similarity means sameness (a major assumption). On the other hand, one would expect distinct groups of saints (church saints and Tribulation saints) to be described in similar ways since they are all saints.

The same holds true for the use of the word *elect*, or *chosen*. Some have concluded that since the elect are mentioned as being in the Tribulation in Matthew 24:22, 24, and 31, then the church will go through the Tribulation. But what elect people are meant? The heathen king Cyrus was called a messiah (Isaiah 45:1). So was Christ (Psalm 2:2). Israel was called God's elect, even though the nation was a mixture of redeemed and unredeemed people (Isaiah 45:4). Christ is also God's elect (Isaiah 42:1). So is the church (Colossians 3:12). So are some angels (1 Timothy 5:21). Not all elect are the same, and the chosen ones of the Tribulation days do not have to be the same as the elect of the church simply because the same term is used of both groups.

How Distinct Is the Church?

Actually, the question boils down to whether the church is a distinct entity in the program of God. Those who emphasize the distinctiveness of the church will be pretribulationists, and those who de-emphasize it will usually be posttribulationists. Distinctiveness here means distinct from Israel. Is the church distinct from Israel? If so, then the church will not be a participant in the Tribulation, since during that time God will be dealing primarily with Israel once again. If the church is a continuation of Israel, then we could more readily conclude that she will experience the Tribulation.

The "mystery" character of the church argues against her being related to Israel and for her being a distinct entity in God's program. God's work in this age of including Jews and Gentiles in the same body is a mystery that was not known in past ages (Ephesians 3:3-6; Colossians 1:26). But the Tribulation was revealed in the Old Testament (Isaiah 24). Furthermore, Daniel's prophecy concerning the 70 weeks of sevens specifically concerned "your people and your holy city" (Daniel 9:24). All 70 weeks relate to Israel. The church had no part in the already-fulfilled 69 weeks and will not be a part of the seventieth week of the future Tribulation. This requires a pretrib rapture.

Of course, other mysteries in the Bible relate to other time periods (such as the mystery of God in Revelation 10:7, which will be consummated in the Tribulation period; and the mystery of the incarnation in 1 Timothy 3:16). To use this as proof that the mystery of the body of Christ cannot be related only to the period from Pentecost to the rapture is fallacious. Clearly, not all biblical mysteries relate to the church age, but that does not prove that one of them does not.

The Resurrection in Revelation 20:4

Sometimes the mention of a resurrection in Revelation 20:4 is used to argue for the posttrib view in this way: The verse says that there will be a resurrection at the conclusion of the Tribulation; the rapture involves a resurrection of the dead; therefore, the rapture is at the conclusion of the Tribulation. One posttribulationist declares that this is the only passage that indicates the time of the rapture; all other passages are only inferences.[1]

Douglas Moo also uses Revelation 20:4 to support a posttrib rapture:

> For these reasons, it is *probable* that Revelation 20:4 depicts the resurrection of all the righteous dead—including church saints. Since the Rapture occurs at the same time as this resurrection [an assumption, since nothing is mentioned in the text about the living being changed], and the first resurrection is clearly posttribulational, the Rapture must also be considered posttribulational (emphasis added).[2]

There are two problems with this conclusion. First, does the presence of some of the same features in two different events prove that they are the same event? Of course not. And second, Revelation 20:4 speaks only of a resurrection of the dead, not of a translation of living people, which is a prominent and vital part of the other descriptions of the rapture in 1 Thessalonians 4:13-18 and 1 Corinthians 15:51-58.

We conclude, then, that neither the use of words like

church or *saints*, nor phrases that describe believers, nor Revelation 20:4, will settle the matter of the timing of the rapture. But the distinctive mystery character of the church, especially in relation to the prophecy of the 70 weeks in Daniel 9, does argue for a pretrib rapture. The arguments posttribulationists use do not show that the body of Christ is on the earth in Revelation 4–18.

8

WHERE DID THE PRETRIB VIEW ORIGINATE?

It is not unusual for people to assume that the antiquity of a doctrine enhances its truthfulness beyond that of a more recent one. Now, of course the history of a doctrine is important. But its importance is mainly in discovering how people formulated it, discussed it, or perverted it. If a doctrine began with the early church, then with all that history behind us, we ought to be expressing it very accurately today. If a doctrine began in recent centuries, then we may properly expect formulation and discussion to be going on today. But to be true, a doctrine must be in the Bible, not simply in church history—past or recent.

Some of the early church fathers taught baptismal regeneration, but that scarcely makes it a true doctrine.

The early church did not spell out a pretrib rapture, but that scarcely makes it an untrue doctrine.

The early church believed in the Tribulation, the imminent coming of Christ, and the Millennium following Christ's return. The early church was clearly premillennial but not clearly pretribulational, nor was it clearly posttribulational when measured against today's developed pre- or posttrib teachings.

Development in eschatology really did not come to preeminence until the modern period of church history, which began after the Reformation. During this period, postmillennialism was first proposed; it then faded, but more recently has had a revival, even claiming as converts some longtime amillennialists. During this same period, amillennialism has flourished, as has premillennialism. Only in the nineteenth and twentieth centuries have the pretrib and posttrib views been systematically expounded.

A systematic posttrib view apparently developed as people began to reject the expanding influence of the pretrib view. That is not to say that all early posttribulationists were first pretribulationists before abandoning that position. Rather, when a more detailed pretrib scheme developed, some reacted to it and began to expound a more detailed posttrib scheme.[1]

Undoubtedly J.N. Darby (1800–1882) gave the greatest initial impetus to the systematic pretrib view as we know it today. Darby, an Englishman, was concerned about the purity of the church—a purity he could not find in the Church of England because of its alliance with the state. That led him to begin meeting with an already-existing group who felt the same way and who gathered for fellowship and deeper Bible study. In time, he saw the church as a special work of God, distinct from His program for Israel. This truth, integrated with his premillennial eschatology, led him to believe that the rapture would occur before the Tribulation and that, during the Tribulation, God would turn again to deal specially with Israel. Those views were accepted and promoted by others, and a systematic posttrib view developed as a reaction against them.

Attempts have been made to discredit Darby's pretrib view by claiming that he did not get it from the Bible but from a heretic and from a mystic.

Edward Irving

The heretic was Edward Irving (1792–1834), who was deposed in 1833 from the Church of Scotland on the charge that he held to the sinfulness of Christ's humanity. Prior to this, manifestations of tongues and healings appeared in his church in London, and his congregation had become a rallying point for millennial expectations.

It is one thing to recognize that the Irvingites were vitally interested in prophecy; it is another thing to claim that they taught a pretrib rapture; and it is quite a different thing to imply that Darby was influenced by them.

At best, the Irvingite eschatology is unclear. One of their group drew a time distinction between the epiphany (the Lord's appearing and rapture) and the *parousia* (the Lord's coming to earth), but it was not seven years. Another placed the rapture at the same time as the last bowl judgment of Revelation 16 (which is the last judgment of the Tribulation period) and *after* the setting up of the ten-nation federation. Still another wrote that the rapture will take place as the Lord is on His way down to earth, which is the typical posttrib position.[2]

The Irvingites obviously did not teach imminency, or that the seventieth week of Daniel would intervene between the rapture and the second advent. These were doctrines that Darby clearly taught in the Powerscourt conference of 1833. A historian puts the matter in proper perspective:

> Darby's opponents claimed that the doctrine [of the rapture] originated in one of the outbursts of tongues in Edward Irving's church about 1832. This seems to be a groundless and pernicious charge. Neither Irving nor any member of the Albury group advocated any doctrine resembling the secret rapture. As we have seen, they were all historicists, looking for the fulfillment of one or another prophecy in the Revelation as the next step in the divine timetable, anticipating the second coming of Christ soon but not immediately.[3]

There is no connection between Darby's pretribulationism and the Irvingite teaching.

Margaret Macdonald

The mystic was an adolescent named Margaret Macdonald (c. 1815–1840), who lived in Port Glasgow, Scotland, and who, it is alleged, influenced both the Irvingites and Darby with regard to a pretrib rapture. That is the charge leveled by Dave MacPherson in *The Incredible Cover-Up.*[4] MacPherson further alleges that Darby not only received his pretrib rapture concept from Miss Macdonald (when she was 15), but that he deliberately hid from his followers where he received it, since she was also involved in speaking in tongues and receiving visions.[5]

Let me quote excerpts from MacPherson's report of Margaret Macdonald's handwritten account of her 1830 pretrib revelation so that we may see if she in fact did teach a pretribulational rapture:

> …the spiritual temple must and shall be reared, and the fullness of Christ be poured into his body, and then shall we be caught up to meet him…The trial of the Church is from Antichrist. It is by being filled with the Spirit that we shall be kept…O it is not known what the sign of the Son of man is…I saw it was just the Lord himself descending from Heaven with a shout…Now will THE WICKED be revealed, with all power and signs and lying wonders, so

that if it were possible the very elect will be deceived—This is the fiery trial which is to try us.[6]

Three things concern me here:

1. This adolescent distinguished spiritual believers from other believers and saw only the spiritual ones participating in the rapture. MacPherson wrongly concludes from this that Macdonald meant to teach a secret coming. In reality, she was teaching the partial-rapture view.

2. She saw the church ("us") being purged by Antichrist. MacPherson reads this to mean that the church will be raptured before Antichrist arises, ignoring the "us."[7] In reality, Macdonald saw the church enduring Antichrist's persecution of the Tribulation days.

3. Macdonald identified the sign of the coming of the Son of man (Matthew 24:30), which clearly appears at the end of the Tribulation as being seen at the same time as the rapture. MacPherson says Macdonald either believed in a very short Tribulation period, or, more likely to him, she understood that the sign would be seen only by Spirit-filled believers before the wicked one was revealed.[8] In reality, Macdonald

revealed by this statement complete confusion. Though taken at face value, her vision equated the sign at the end of the Tribulation with the rapture—hardly pretribulationism!

As for the young and chronically ill Margaret Macdonald, we would have to call her a "confused rapturist." She held to elements of the partial rapture, the posttrib view, perhaps the midtrib view, but never the pretrib view.

By Darby's own testimony, his ideas came from the Bible, particularly his understanding of the distinctiveness of the church (in 1826–1828). His belief that the rapture would be a considerable time before the second coming was developed by 1830, and the concept of a parenthesis between the sixty-ninth and seventieth weeks of Daniel no later than 1833. He seemed to be unsettled about the secret aspect of the rapture as late as the 1840s.[9]

These are the essential facts concerning the history of the modern pretrib view. Actually, both the systematic pre- and posttrib views are recent developments, since the church did not study the field of eschatology until after the Reformation.[10]

POPULATING THE MILLENNIAL KINGDOM

When the Millennium begins, some people have to be alive in unresurrected bodies in order to beget children and populate that kingdom. All premillennialists agree with this.

The Millennium not only involves the reign of Jesus Christ with His people, who will then have resurrected bodies—it also includes His reign over people on this earth who will not have resurrected bodies. If there were only resurrected saints in the millennial kingdom, then there would be no death, no increase in population, and no differences in the ages of millennial citizens (all of which are indicated as characterizing the kingdom—Isaiah 65:20; Zechariah 8:5; Revelation 20:8). Since resurrected people do not propagate, there would be no way to populate this kingdom unless some unresurrected people enter the Millennium. Thus all premillennialists see the need to have some adults who survive the Tribulation. They will not be taken to heaven at the end of the Tribulation, but rather, they will enter the Millennium in unresurrected bodies to become the first parents of the millennial population.

The Pretrib Population

The pretrib understanding of future events satisfies this need easily. The rapture will occur before the Tribulation, removing all the redeemed who are living on the earth at that time. But many people will be saved during the Tribulation (Revelation 7:9, 14), including a specific group of 144,000 Jewish people (Revelation 7:4). Of those saved during that horrible time, many will be martyred (Revelation 6:11; 13:15), but some will survive to enter the Millennium (Matthew 25:34; Zechariah 14:11). The initial group that enters the Millennium will not only enter with natural bodies, they will also be redeemed people who willingly submit to the rule of the King. In due time, babies will be born and grow up. Some will receive Christ into their hearts; others will not. But all will have to give allegiance to the King's government or be punished. By the end of the Millennium, there will be innumerable rebels who will have given outward obedience to the King but who, when given the opportunity by Satan after his release, will join his revolution against Christ (Revelation 20:7-9).

Thus in the pretrib understanding of these future events, the original parents in the millennial kingdom will come from the redeemed (but unresurrected) survivors of the Tribulation. They will be the sheep of Matthew 25:34, and the faithful Jewish survivors of Ezekiel 20:38.

The Posttrib Population

In contrast stands the posttrib picture. The church, of course, will live through the Tribulation. Though some believers will be martyred, many will be protected and survive. The 144,000 Jews and the great multitude of Revelation 7 are included in the church. At the end of the Tribulation all living believers will be raptured, given resurrection bodies, and return immediately to earth in the single event of the rapture and second coming. This would seem to eliminate all redeemed, unresurrected people from the earth at that point in time so that there would be no one left to populate the millennial kingdom. If the wicked survivors are either killed or consigned to Hades at the end of the Tribulation, then there will be no one left in an unresurrected body to enter the Millennium.

So, either the posttribulationist must find some people who will not be saved when the rapture begins but who will be saved at the instantaneous rapture/second coming event; or, he must allow the initial parents in the Millennium to be unsaved people who somehow are not killed or judged at or after Armageddon. Those are the only options by which the posttribulationist can find millennial parents.

The First Millennial Generation

We need to be reminded of another detail: The millennial population will include both Jewish and Gentile people (Isaiah 19:24-25). So the first generation must be made up of both. But a posttrib rapture will remove all the potentially redeemed millennial parents of every race. And the judgments of the second coming will remove all the potentially unredeemed millennial parents of every race. Where, then, will those parents come from?

Most posttribulationists do not attempt an answer to this question. This may be because they do not usually put the details of their system together in an orderly way. Their picture of the future is painted with broad strokes, not fine detail. Posttribulationists do not sponsor prophecy conferences in which their speakers are expected to describe rather specifically the system they promote. As a result, some posttribulationists may not have thought about this question.

Robert Gundry is an exception.[1] His answer is twofold. The Jewish progenitors of the millennial population will come from the 144,000, who will not be saved at any time *during* the Tribulation but only at the end.[2] The Gentile parents will come from the wicked who will somehow escape death or judgment at the end of the Tribulation.[3] Those wicked are the ones left in Matthew 24:40-41 (in contrast to the ones taken in the posttrib rapture). He says that "a partial destruction would leave the remaining unsaved to populate the millennial earth."[4] By the way, if those left for judgment involve only part of the wicked, perhaps those taken in the rapture will include only part of the redeemed. That parallelism would give us a new view: the partial-posttrib rapture!

Furthermore, if the posttrib picture is correct, an adjustment has to be made in the time of the judgment of the sheep and goats in Matthew 25:31-46. The reason is simple: If the rapture occurs after the Tribulation, then all the sheep (redeemed) will have been removed from the earth; thus, there would be no sheep to be part of that judgment if it occurs at the second coming, which is said to be a single event with the rapture. There is no way the rapture can remove the sheep and yet have them present on the earth immediately following the rapture to be judged. So either the rapture cannot be a posttrib one, or the judgment of the sheep and goats must occur after the second coming (Gundry places it after the Millennium).

We need to examine three things that are necessary to the posttrib answer: 1) the conversion of the 144,000,

2) the identification of the groups in Matthew 24:40-41, and 3) the time of the judgment of the sheep and goats in Matthew 25:31-46.

The 144,000 Jews

Some posttribulationists consider the 144,000 Jews to be "spiritual Israel—the church."[5] If so, then their sealing is at the beginning of the Tribulation and relates to their spiritual salvation as well as to their physical protection. Gundry acknowledges that the 144,000 might belong to the church (and therefore be saved at the beginning).

But he prefers to regard them as unsaved throughout the Tribulation and identical with the group that will look on Christ when He returns (Zechariah 12:10) and with the Israel who will be saved at the second coming (Romans 11:26-27).

Gundry's preference is a logical one. If the 144,000 were saved anytime during the Tribulation years—at the beginning, in the middle, or during the last year—they would be taken in the posttrib rapture, given resurrection bodies at that time, and then return at the same time to reign with Christ in the kingdom. But resurrection bodies preclude their being the parents of anybody in the kingdom. On the other hand, if they were not saved until the very end of the second coming, they would "escape" the rapture and stay converted, but they would remain in unresurrected bodies and thus be able to become parents of millennial children.

Pretribulationists believe that there will be a group of Jewish people converted at the conclusion of the Tribulation who will become the parents of the Jewish portion of the millennial population. They will come from among the Jewish people who survive the Tribulation, even though they were unsaved throughout it. When the Lord returns, they will be gathered and judged; the rebels (possibly two thirds, Zechariah 13:8) will be excluded from the kingdom, and those who turn in faith when they see Him will enter the kingdom (Ezekiel 20:33-44). Those believing survivors constitute the "all" of "all Israel" that will be saved at the second coming (Romans 11:26). But they will not be given resurrection bodies at that time; rather, they will enter the kingdom in material bodies with the ability to propagate.

Why can't the posttribulationist let this group be the millennial parents? Because that group will believe only when they see the Lord coming at the posttrib rapture. So they also would be raptured, taken to heaven, given resurrection bodies, and thus be unable to parent. The rapture, whenever it occurs, will be the greatest separation of believers from unbelievers imaginable; so if there is to be a group of Jewish people who will believe when they see the Lord coming, and if that coming is the posttribulational rapture/second coming, then they will be raptured because at that moment they will become believers. So the post-tribulationist needs to have a group that is sealed in an unsaved state long enough to miss the rapture but not long enough to miss entering the Millennium in material bodies. Thus, as one would expect, Gundry says of Ezekiel 20 that "that passage may not portray a formal judgment at all."[6] Actually, it cannot, in the posttrib system.

Can the 144,000 be considered unconverted throughout the Tribulation years? Yes, they can. One can hold any interpretation one wishes. The question is not, Is it possible to interpret them that way? The question is, Is it reasonable to do so? What does the text of Revelation 7:1-8 say?

It states two significant facts: the 144,000 "have the seal of the living God" (verse 2), and they are "the bondservants of our God" (verse 3). The text does not specifically say *what* their service is, but it does say *whom* they serve. They serve God, not Antichrist. Are we to imagine that a group of 144,000 unsaved people are called God's bondservants? Posttribulationists weakly explain that the designation is anticipatory of their millennial service, when they will have been converted. This explanation is possible; but is it the most likely meaning of the text? I don't think so.

Even if the designation "bondservants of our God" does not apply to the 144,000 in the Tribulation but only in the Millennium, the statement in verse 2 is very difficult to harmonize with the posttrib system. The group is said to be sealed before the Tribulation judgments begin (verse 1). To fit this into the posttrib view, you would need a distinct group of unconverted Jewish people on whose foreheads God has placed His seal. As unsaved people, they (or surely some of them) would follow Antichrist, who will place his mark on their foreheads or hands. And the destiny of Antichrist's followers *has already been predetermined*: They will be tormented forever with fire and brimstone (Revelation 14:9-11). None of his followers will be saved, not even 144,000 of them.

To sum up, the posttrib view needs to have an unconverted group of Jews survive the Tribulation, but who, because they are unconverted, will not be raptured at the end, but who will be converted by the time the Millennium begins so they can enter the Millennium in their unresurrected bodies and beget children. The only group that can qualify is the 144,000—assuming they can be described as unconverted servants of God who have God's seal on their foreheads before the Tribulation begins, and who do not follow Antichrist so they will not have his mark. Is all this really possible?

Who's "Taken," and Where?

Not only must the 144,000 be identified in a particular

way, the groups distinguished in Matthew 24:40-41 must also be identified in a certain way in order to come up with the posttrib picture.

According to the posttrib understanding, Matthew 24:40 teaches the following: "Then [at the posttrib rapture/second coming] there shall be two men in the field; one [saved, representing the church] will be taken [in the posttrib rapture], and one [unsaved, representing the wicked] will be left [for judgment, though not all will be judged, so some will be left to be parents of the Gentile population of the Millennium]." And the same for verse 41: The one taken is raptured, and the one left is judged.

By contrast, the pretribulationist sees the verses as a general statement of the results of the specific judgments on surviving Jews and Gentiles at the second coming. Those who are taken are taken into the judgments and condemned. Those who are left successfully pass the judgments, and are left for blessing in the kingdom.

The posttribulationist must add the stipulation that not all who are left will be judged and condemned, so that there will be some left to populate the earth. But therein lies an inconsistency: The rapture will take all the redeemed, but the judgment will not include all the unredeemed. Only part of the wicked will be judged.

The two interpretations look like this:

	Pretribulational Interpretation	Posttribulational Interpretation
"Taken"	Into judgment	Into heaven in the posttribulational rapture
"Left"	For blessing in the kingdom (in unresurrected bodies to propagate)	For judgment (but only part will be judged so the rest can enter the kingdom in unresurrected bodies)

Pretribulationists support their view by pointing out that according to verse 39, the Flood took the people of Noah's day into judgment; therefore, those taken at the second coming will also be taken into judgment.

Posttribulationists observe that a different word is used in verse 39 for "took away" than in verses 40-41, indicating two different kinds of taking away—verse 39 into judgment, but verses 40-41 into heaven at the rapture. They reinforce this argument by pointing out that the word in verses 40-41 is the same word used to describe the rapture in John 14:3, "receive you to Myself."

Pretribulationists note that in John 19:16 that same word used in Matthew 24:40-41 (supposedly of the rapture according to posttribulationists) is used of taking the Lord into judgment, so obviously it could mean judgment in Matthew 24:40-41, as the pretrib view teaches. Again, as we saw in an earlier chapter, a back-and-forth discussion of some words is inconclusive.

Nevertheless, the debate is not without resolution. It can be settled by looking at the parallel passage in Luke 17:34-37, where the same warning about ones being taken and left is given by the Lord. However, Luke adds a question asked by the disciples: "Where, Lord?" They asked Him where those taken would be taken. They did not inquire where those left would be left. If the Lord intended us to understand that those taken would be taken in the rapture (as the posttrib view teaches), He should have answered the question by saying heaven, or the Father's house, or some similar expression. But His answer conveyed that they would be taken somewhere quite opposite of bliss. His answer was, "Where the body is, there will also the vultures be gathered." Christ's answer is a proverb about vultures appearing out of nowhere when an animal dies. Where will they be taken? Where there is death and corruption, not life and immortality. The reference is not to heaven, but to judgment. Thus the pretribulationist's understanding of the identity of the one taken and the one left is the correct one, according to Luke 17:37. A posttrib rapture is not indicated in these verses.

The Sheep and the Goats— Matthew 25:31-46

This judgment of the sheep and goats, placed at the second coming by pretribulationists, has to be moved to a later time if the posttrib view is to be consistent. The reason is that if the rapture occurs at the end of the Tribulation—that is, at the second coming—and if all the sheep are taken to heaven in that rapture, how will there be any left to be assembled before Christ when He comes? They will already have gone. To put it another way: The rapture/second coming will separate the redeemed from the wicked; yet this judgment at the second coming will do the same, only there will not be any righteous on the earth to separate, since they will just have been raptured.

Moving this judgment also provides for unsaved survivors of the Tribulation and second coming to enter the Millennium in unresurrected bodies. Gundry admits, "We are therefore forced to put the judgment of the nations after the Millennium."[7] Forced? Why? Because there cannot be only a partial condemnation of the goats: The text says "all" will be judged. In his interpretation of those who will be left in Matthew 24:40-41, Gundry says that represented only "a partial destruction,"[8] but here, all are specifically said to be involved (Matthew 25:32).

No text requires that there be unsaved people entering

the Millennium. After a few years have passed there will be people, born during the early days of the Millennium, who will grow to adulthood and reject the Savior-King in their hearts (though outwardly obeying Him). But no text requires that there be unsaved people among the survivors of the Tribulation who enter the Millennium. Zechariah 14:16 (sometimes used to support this idea) refers to the first generation of millennial citizens who come through the judgments as redeemed, not as rebels, and who will voluntarily go to Jerusalem to worship the King. But verses 17-21 move on to describe conditions throughout the Millennium, not just at the beginning. As time goes on, some will not obey the King, and they will have to be punished.

Perhaps the more compelling posttrib reason for moving this judgment to the end of the Millennium is not to get goats into the Millennium as much as it is to get sheep into the judgment itself. Let me press the point again: If the judgment occurs at the second coming, and if the rapture has just occurred as part of the second coming, and if the rapture has removed the sheep (as it would), then where will the sheep come from to be present in this judgment?

If, however, the judgment can be moved to the close of the Millennium, then of course there will be both righteous and wicked people living at the conclusion of the Millennium. But how, then, does one reconcile the rather diverse characteristics of Matthew 25:31-46 with those that describe what would supposedly be the same judgment at the great white throne in Revelation 20:11-15? Notice some of the contrasts between the judgment of the sheep and the goats with the judgment at the great white throne.

Gundry calls the judgment of the sheep and goats a "pattern for the general judgment at the end of time."[9] If it is a pattern, it is rather inexact! To be sure, passages describing the same event do not each have to contain all the same details, but these two passages seem to be entirely dissimilar in their details.

If the judgment of the sheep and goats is to be moved to the end of the Millennium, then of course Matthew 25:31 must be understood as referring to the second coming, and verse 32 to the end of the Millennium, 1,000 years later. In other words, the gap of the 1,000-year Millennium must come between verses 31 and 32. Premillennialists recognize that such gaps occur in Scripture (Isaiah 9:6 and John 5:28-29, for example). So this is not an impossible idea, but is it the likely interpretation?

Verses 35-40 give the answer. Do these verses describe millennial conditions? They have to, if this judgment is to occur after the conclusion of the Millennium. If they do, then the Millennium will have to be a time when Christ and His followers are hungry, thirsty, naked, sick, and in prison. Those who disobey the King during the Millennium may be imprisoned, but the text says that during the period preceding the judgment, Christ's followers will be in prison. As certainly as this will not be true during the Millennium, it will be true during the Tribulation. Christ's followers will be hungry, thirsty, naked, sick, and imprisoned during the Tribulation years, but not during the Millennium, when Christ will be ruling in righteousness.

Clearly then, verses 35-40 preclude inserting a gap of 1,000 years between verses 31 and 32. The judgment will immediately follow the coming of Christ, and it will test people on the basis of their heart reaction to conditions during the Tribulation—conditions that will not be present during the Millennium for Christ's followers.

Where, then, has the discussion led us? To the conclusion that the posttrib view cannot answer the question, Who will be the parents of the millennial population? To be sure, those who hold to the posttrib view offer some interesting thinking on the subject. They think the 144,000 will be the Jewish parents; but in order to qualify, they will have to remain unconverted throughout the Tribulation as well as through the rapture/second coming, and then be converted. They think that some of the ones left in the separation of Matthew 24:40-41 will be the Gentile parents (others will be condemned to hell). But this twists the meaning of "taken" and "left," making the taking to heaven in the rapture contrary to the clear meaning of "taken" in Luke 17:36. And to make these ideas consistent, the judgment of the sheep and goats must be placed at the conclusion of the Millennium, and Matthew 25:35-40 must describe millennial conditions.

How much simpler *not* to have to place the rapture at the conclusion of the Tribulation. That allows for people to accept or reject Christ during the Tribulation. Some of these people (none of whom will be raptured, because the rapture will already have occurred) will survive that time to be judged at the second coming (both living Jews and Gentiles). Those who pass those judgments successfully— as redeemed people—will go into the kingdom in earthly bodies to become the first generation of the millennial population, parents of the next generation.

Sheep and Goats	Great White Throne
No resurrection (though Old Testament saints may be raised at the second coming, they will not be part of the judgment)	Resurrection of the dead
No books opened	Books opened
The word *nations* used (and the word is never used of the dead)	The word *dead* used
Sheep present	Righteous not mentioned as present

Sheep and Goats	Great White Throne
Three groups mentioned: sheep, goats, brethren	Only one group mentioned: the dead
Reward is the kingdom and eternal life	No mention of reward, only condemnation
Occurs at the place Christ comes to (i.e., the earth)	Earth has fled away

10

THE DAY OF THE LORD

Pre- and posttribulationists agree that the question of the Day of the Lord bears directly on the time of the rapture. More specifically, the question is about when the Day of the Lord begins. If it begins at the second coming of Christ, then the rapture (which must precede the Day of the Lord) could be (but does not have to be) posttribulational. If the Day of the Lord begins at the middle of the Tribulation, then the rapture would be a midtrib one. But if the Day of the Lord begins at the start of the Tribulation, then the rapture must precede the Tribulation.

In the Bible, the Day of the Lord always involves the broad concept of God's special intervention in human history. The concept includes three facets: 1) a historical facet about God's intervention in Israel's affairs (Joel 1:15; Zephaniah 1:14-18) and in the affairs of heathen nations (Isaiah

13:6; Jeremiah 46:10; Ezekiel 30:3); 2) an illustrative facet, in which a historical incident of God's intervention also illustrates a future intervention (Isaiah 13:6-13; Joel 2:1-11); 3) an eschatological facet about God's intervention in human history in the future (Isaiah 2:12-19; 4:1; 19:23-25; Jeremiah 30:7-9). Only this third, the eschatological facet, pertains to our discussion of the rapture's timing.

All premillennialists agree that the Day of the Lord includes the events of the second coming and the literal 1,000-year Millennium to follow. Premillennialists do not debate when the Day of the Lord will end, only when it will begin.

The posttrib scheme is this: The Day of the Lord will not begin until the judgments of Armageddon are poured out at the conclusion of the Tribulation. The rapture, which precedes the Day of the Lord, will occur at the end of the Tribulation, just before Armageddon, rescuing the church from God's wrath, which will fall at Armageddon.

Two questions now arise. First, how can the rapture precede Armageddon and yet be a single event with the second coming, which puts a stop to Armageddon? Armageddon is not a single, confined battle; it is a war (Revelation 16:14). For the church to miss Armageddon, the rapture cannot be a single, continuous event with the second coming. It would have to be separated by at least a little time. And if it is separated by any time at all, then it is not a posttrib rapture. Second, if the Day of the Lord commences with the judgments at the end of the Tribulation, then how can it begin with a time of peace and safety (1 Thessalonians 5:2-3)? Even a superficial knowledge of the Tribulation does not give the impression that there will be any time of peace and safety, except perhaps at the very beginning—certainly not at the end.

To try to alleviate the tensions raised by these two questions, posttribulationists 1) propose a certain chronology of the judgments described in Revelation, and 2) suggest a most unusual interpretation of 1 Thessalonians 5:2-3 ("peace and safety").

The Judgments of Revelation

The three series of judgments described in Revelation will take place during the Tribulation years. They are revealed under seven seals (chapter 6), seven trumpets (chapters 8–9), and seven bowls (chapter 16). Commentators differ on their understanding of the relation of these judgments to each other. Some believe that they are consecutive—that is, the trumpets follow the seals, and the bowls follow the trumpets. In other words, the first seal judgment will take place shortly after the beginning of the Tribulation, and the last bowl judgment will occur at the end. However, that does not mean that all the judgments in between are evenly spaced throughout the seven years. The seven bowls, for example, will apparently follow each other in quick succession. But overall, the judgments are consecutive.

Others believe that the judgments will be somewhat concurrent—that is, the seventh seal describes the end of the Tribulation, so the seventh trumpet and the seven bowls are all at the end.

Pretribulationists hold to either chronology, but post-tribulationists are better served by holding to the second. The reason: The church, according to the posttrib view, will escape God's wrath, which will come only at the very end of the Tribulation. The sixth seal and the sixth and seventh bowls predict wrath, so they must come at the very end. "Thus, God's wrath will not stretch throughout the whole tribulation. Those passages in Revelation which speak of divine wrath deal, rather, with the close of the tribulation."[1]

Posttribulationists not only limit the wrath of God to the very end of the Tribulation, but they also teach that it will be poured out only on the unregenerate.

Posttrib Assumptions

Let us examine some of the necessary assumptions for such a view.

To say that God's wrath is directed only against the unregenerate is one thing; but to imply that the regenerate are protected from any of its effects is to add something that may not be true. For example, there is not only this future outpouring of God's wrath, but there is also a present wrath (Romans 1:18). It is directed against unbelievers and results in all kinds of perverse and corrupt activities, including false philosophies, homosexuality, murder, and so on. The wrath of God is on unbelievers, but does it follow that believers are now protected from the effects of these activities? Of course not. The unbeliever who commits murder may murder a believer, for example.

Likewise, in connection with the future wrath of God, it does not follow that when God pours out the judgments of His wrath, believers will escape the effects of those judgments, even though they will be directed against unbelievers. While the posttrib view tries to throw a mantle of safety over believers to protect them from the effects of God's coming wrath, that does not accord with what is true of His wrath and its effects today.

But believers will be rescued, says the posttribulationist, because they will be raptured before that wrath is poured out on unbelievers. "Not until the final crisis at Armageddon, when Jesus descends [and the Church is caught up, if posttribulationism be correct], will God pour out His wrath upon the unregenerate."[2] However, Armageddon is not a single battle but the climax of a war. So to miss the wrath of God, believers would have to be raptured before Christ descends to end the campaign of Armageddon.

Notice, too, that Revelation 6:17 announces that the wrath "has come." That verb tense seems to indicate that the wrath already has been poured out, and that it did not just begin with the sixth seal. Therefore, the verse seems

to say that the wrath will start before the end of the Tribulation. To counter the force of this, posttribulationists
have the verb tense as meaning that the wrath is on the
verge of breaking forth—that is, it will not have started
before the very end.[3] Now this is a possible use of that
verb tense, but it is highly unlikely in this verse. As Henry
Alford indicates, the "virtually *perfect* sense of the aorist
elthen here can hardly be questioned."[4] He explains this
sense of the verb as "alluding to the result of the whole
series of events past, and not to be expressed in English
except by a perfect."[5]

Thus, supported by reputable scholarship, the meaning of this verse is *not* that God's wrath is on the verge of
being poured out (as posttribulationists *must* understand
it, or spoil the system), but that the wrath has already been
poured out with continuing results.

This argument about the meaning of the verb tense
is also used by the relatively new pre-wrath rapture view.
However, this teaching places the rapture three-quarters
of the way through the seven-year Tribulation period and
before the pouring out of God's wrath on the earth. It
states that the rapture, the beginning of the Day of the
Lord, and the pouring out of God's wrath will all occur
three-fourths of the way through the Tribulation. This
places these events at Revelation 8:1, the opening of the
seventh seal.[6]

While the verb tense in Revelation 6:17 may mean "is

about to come," this is not the way John uses it in other places in Revelation. In 11:18; 14:7, 15; 18:10; and 19:7, the same verb in the same tense as in 6:17 is used of events and people that are present and already on the scene, not that are about to come in the (however near) future.

The question of whether the three series of judgments in Revelation are successive or recapitulating (or a combination) may never be decided with finality. But if one sees much succession, then the posttrib picture is blurred accordingly. The more the judgments can be clustered at the very end, the clearer the posttrib picture.

At best, however, the picture is confused. The Day of the Lord, according to posttribulationists, includes the final judgment of Armageddon;[7] and yet, "clearly, the day of the Lord will not begin with the tribulation or any part of it."[8] At the same time, "those passages in Revelation which speak of divine wrath deal...with the close of the tribulation."[9]

To sum up the posttribulationist's position here: The rapture can precede Armageddon—when the wrath of God will be poured out and when the Day of the Lord will begin—*if* many of the judgments of Revelation are bunched together at the end, as simultaneous as possible, *and if* the verb tense in Revelation 6:17 has a special meaning, *and if* the effects of the outpouring of God's wrath do not have any fallout on believers, *and if* the final conflict is a single battle, not a war with multiple battles.

The Time of Peace and Safety

A second question posttribulationists must answer is, How can the Day of the Lord begin with a time of peace and safety if it begins with the wrath of God poured out at Armageddon?

Paul wrote, "You yourselves know full well that the day of the Lord will come just like a thief in the night. While they are saying, 'Peace and safety!' then destruction will come upon them suddenly like birth pangs upon a woman with child; and they shall not escape" (1 Thessalonians 5:2-3). The coming, or beginning, of the Day of the Lord will occur during a time of peace. It may be a secure or insecure peace, but it will not be a time of war and conflict. The description scarcely seems to fit the end of the Tribulation, when "all nations" will converge on Israel (Zechariah 12:3; 14:2; Revelation 16:14). How, then, can the posttrib scheme be correct?

The chronology in 1 Thessalonians 5:2-3 is clear: peace at the beginning of the Day of the Lord, followed by sudden destruction. But the posttrib view has already declared that the Day of the Lord will not begin with the Tribulation or any part of it. Does this mean that it will begin with the establishment of Christ's kingdom? That period will certainly be one of peace and safety. But if the chronology is followed, then the Millennium will experience catastrophic destruction shortly after it begins!

Actually, the Day of the Lord begins just before

Armageddon, according to the posttrib view, when the wrath of God will be poured out. How will it be preceded by a time of peace? Two answers have been suggested.

1. "Perhaps just before Armageddon there will be a lull, a seeming end of world upheavals, which will excite men's hopes for the peace which has so long eluded them."[10] Of course such a "lull" is not even hinted at in the text. Even if one could imagine a lull in the military conflicts during the concluding months of the Tribulation, how could it be said that people will experience safety when so many physical upheavals will be reshaping the earth?

   The last judgments of each of the series in Revelation reveals killing of martyrs (6:9), a meteor shower (6:13), earthquakes (6:14), torment like the sting of a scorpion (9:10), one-third of the population killed (9:18), people gnawing their tongues because of pain (16:10), armies converging on Armageddon (16:14), and widespread destruction (16:20-21). And remember that according to posttribulationists, some, if not all, of these judgments will occur toward the end of the Tribulation. And yet somewhere during this time, when these events will be taking place, there will be a lull that will enable people to feel that they are in a time of peace and safety.

2. An alternate suggestion offers a novel interpretation of 1 Thessalonians 5:2: "However, Paul did not write, 'When there shall *be* peace and safety,' but rather, 'While they are *saying...*' The very form of the statement suggests that peace and safety will not be the actual condition of the world preceding the Day of the Lord, but the expressed *wish* and/or *expectation* of men which God will answer with a blow of judgment."[11]

This is novel because the passage contrasts peace and safety with destruction. If peace and safety are merely a wish in the midst of war and danger, then any contrast with destruction that will follow disappears.

Posttrib Logjam

The posttrib view has a veritable logjam at the second coming of Christ. This eschatological logjam includes: a number of the judgments occurring then, the rapture occurring then as a part of the second coming, God's wrath being held off until then, a time of peace and safety, the Day of the Lord beginning with those judgments, and yet not including any part of the Tribulation!

Is there any way to unravel this confusion? Certainly, and it is simply by having time between the rapture and the second coming. How much time? More time than the posttribulationists allow for, which is none; and more time than the midtribulationists allow, unless the first half of the Tribulation contains no judgments. In other words, we need as much time as the pretrib view has.

We know when peace will cease. Peace will be taken from the earth when the second seal judgment occurs (Revelation 6:4). No posttrib scheme that I know places this at the end of the Tribulation. This must occur near the beginning of that awful period. And likewise, the Day of the Lord must begin by that time as well.

The Lord taught this same sequence of events in the Olivet Discourse. He predicted that wars, famines, and earthquakes will occur before Antichrist establishes himself in the Temple, demanding to be worshipped. That event will occur at the midpoint of the Tribulation, but wars will characterize the entire time. Again, we arrive at the same conclusion: The Day of the Lord begins at the start of the Tribulation, just after a time of peace and safety.

Paul set down the same chronology in 2 Thessalonians 2:1-3. He assured the Thessalonians that the Day of the Lord was not yet upon them because two things would have to occur first: apostasy and the revelation of the man of sin. Both events will occur before the Day of the Lord begins, according to the posttrib teaching that the Day of the Lord does not begin until the end of the Tribulation. But the two events also fit the pretrib understanding of the future. The apostasy is agelong and will climax even before the church is removed from the world. The man of sin will be revealed when he signs the treaty with Israel (Daniel 9:27). The signing of that treaty signals the beginning of the Day of the Lord, and that is at the beginning of the seventieth week, at the beginning of the Tribulation. The treaty will add to the general feeling that peace has been achieved. But the peace will be short-lived.

Furthermore, Paul taught that the man of sin cannot be revealed until a certain restraint is removed. Apart from discussing the identity of the restrainer, let us simply ask two questions of the posttribulationist's understanding here.

First, if the church is to go through the Tribulation, and if during that time multitudes are converted, added to the church, and protected until the rapture, will not the church be a mightier force in this world than ever before? Wouldn't such a church—enlarged, sealed, protected, empowered, and preserved during the Tribulation—be such a restraint on the man of sin that he could hardly be as unrestrained as the Bible pictures him?

Second, if the Thessalonians were agitated because they thought the Day of the Lord had come and they were already in it, then how could Paul comfort them by assuring them that they were not in it, but would be as soon as the man of sin came on the scene? What comfort is there in assuring people that they will live through the career of the man of sin before they will be raptured?

So we arrive at the same conclusion: The Day of the Lord will begin as soon as the man of sin is revealed, and that will happen at the beginning of the Tribulation, not at the end.

1 Thessalonians 4 and 5

In 1 Thessalonians 4:13-18, Paul tried to allay the fear of some Thessalonians that their deceased believers might not share in the coming kingdom. He assured them that the dead will be raised and the living changed at the church's catching away. That was something about which they were uninformed (verse 13), even though he had taught them about future things during his short ministry among them (2 Thessalonians 2:5).

In 1 Thessalonians 5:1-11, Paul wrote concerning the beginning of the Day of the Lord. In a time of peace and safety, it will come unexpectedly and terrifyingly, with pain (verse 3) and wrath (verse 9). In the meantime, believers are to live alert and sober. The exhortations of verses 6, 8, 9, and 10 are not to watch for signs during the Tribulation (in preparation for the Day of the Lord at the end), but to godly living in view of the coming Tribulation, which believers will escape (see 1 Corinthians 15:58). Of this teaching Paul said they were fully aware (verse 1). How could that be? Partly from his own teaching, but more from their knowledge of the Old Testament.

In the Old Testament, the Day of the Lord is referred to by that phrase about 20 times, often with eschatological implications. In addition, a parallel term, "the last days," occurs 14 times, always eschatological. Further, the phrase "in that day" occurs over a 100 times and is generally eschatological. In Isaiah 2:2, 11-12 (KJV), the three phrases refer to the same eschatological time. So there was ample reason for Paul to say that his readers knew about the Day of the Lord from the Old Testament itself.

But concerning the rapture, there is no Old Testament revelation. This omission from over 100 passages seems hard to understand if the rapture is the first event of the Day of the Lord, as the posttrib view teaches. But if the rapture is a mystery unrevealed in the Old Testament, and if it precedes the beginning of the Day of the Lord, as pretribulationists teach, then it is not strange that Paul had to inform them about the rapture.

Posttribulationists, then, want to make a very close connection between 4:13-18 and 5:1-11, whereas pretribulationists are better served by seeing a contrast of subjects between the two passages.

Thus the posttrib scenario runs like this: Paul moves with ease from his discussion of the rapture in 4:13-18 to the discussion of the *parousia* in 5:1-11 because he is talking about events that occur at the same time and not events separated by seven years. Paul's choice of *de* (the first Greek word in 5:1), a simple connective with only a slight contrastive sense, indicates this close connection. And since the Day of the Lord will not begin until the second coming, the rapture will occur then also.[12]

Pretribulationists point out that the contrast between the two subjects is sharpened by the fact that Paul did not simply use the word *de* to begin 5:1, but a phrase, *peri de*. This is very significant. Elsewhere in his writings, Paul uses *peri de* to denote a new and contrasting subject: 1 Corinthians 7:1, 25; 8:1; 12:1; 16:1, 12; 1 Thessalonians 4:9; 5:1. The posttrib contention that the same subject is being discussed in 4:13-18 and 5:1-11 might be supported by the use of *de* alone, but it is completely nullified by the use of *peri de*. So the pretrib use of the passage is strongly supported exegetically. The rapture is not a part of the Day of the Lord and therefore cannot occur posttrib.

Clearly, the question about the beginning of the Day of the Lord is a watershed issue between pre- and posttribulationists. Pretribulationists see the Day of the Lord beginning at the start of the Tribulation for the following reasons:

1. The very first judgments (by whatever chronology one uses) include war, famine, and the death of one-fourth of the earth's population.

2. The only time the Bible mentions peace and safety during the Tribulation period is at the very beginning. This time will be followed immediately by war, destruction, and upheavals that will continue unabated until Jesus Christ returns. Thus, the Day of the Lord must begin at the start of the Tribulation, and the rapture must be before it.

3. The revelation of the man of sin will occur at the beginning of the Tribulation, when he makes a pact with the Jewish people.

4. The much more normal understanding of the verb in Revelation 6:17 conveys the idea that the wrath has already come and continues.

5. Paul's use of *peri de,* not simply *de,* in 1 Thessalonians 5:1 indicates contrasting subjects.

6. The removal of peace from the earth just after the Tribulation begins fits only the pretrib view.

For the posttrib view to be correct, it must provide much more satisfactory answers to the following questions:

1. How can the Day of the Lord not begin with the Tribulation or any part of it, and yet begin with the judgments of Armageddon?

2. How can the final conflict at the end of the

Tribulation be shrunk into a single battle of short enough duration so that the church can be raptured before it starts (in order to escape the wrath), and yet turn right around and accompany Christ on His return to earth?

3. Does believers' protection from the wrath poured out on unbelievers really include their exemption from the fallout effects of the actions of those unbelievers on whom the wrath is poured? It does not today. Why would we expect it to in the future?

4. How does bunching the wrath judgments at the end of the Tribulation take care of the problem that equally severe judgments seem to take place earlier in the Tribulation, and fall on believers as well as unbelievers?

5. What is the more normal interpretation of the aorist in Revelation 6:17?

6. Does not the use of the phrase *peri de* in 1 Thessalonians 5:1 indicate that the rapture is not a part of the Day of the Lord at the end of the Tribulation?

Only the pretrib view fits harmoniously with all the scriptural evidence and answers those questions satisfactorily.

11

WRATH OR RAPTURE?

If wrath seems to characterize more of the Tribulation period than just the last crisis, then either the church 1) must endure that wrath, or 2) be raptured out of it beforehand, or 3) be protected somehow during the Tribulation.

Option number one is not held by either pre- or posttribulationists (partial rapturists hold it). Pretribulationists opt for the second, and posttribulationists for the third.

Wrath or Wraths?

To strengthen their case for removing the church from Tribulation wrath, posttribulationists catalog the troubles of that time into three wraths: the wrath of Satan, the wrath of wicked men (both of which the church will experience), and the wrath of God (which will come only at the very end, from which the church will be delivered).

Posttribulationists point out that the word *wrath* is used in Revelation for God's wrath against the wicked, and that the word *tribulation* refers to the saints' persecution during the seven years. But that distinction does not also prove that God's wrath is limited to the very end, or that it does not include the activities of Satan, Antichrist, or sinners.[1] God's wrath at Armageddon (Revelation 19:15) will include the activities of Satan and demons (Revelation 16:13-14). His wrath poured out in the bowl judgments will affect a place (the earth), and not just wicked people (Revelation 16:1).

The righteous cannot be protected from all the fallout effects of the wraths of the Tribulation period. By no chronology can all the seal, trumpet, and bowl judgments be relegated to the end of the Tribulation, nor is there any way to protect the righteous from worldwide war, famine, and earthquakes, for example. Indeed, we know that many righteous will be martyred throughout the period, which means they will not be protected (Revelation 6:10-11).

During the Tribulation, there will be wrath and wraths from many quarters, falling everywhere, and affecting everyone in some way or another.

When Will God's Wrath Fall?

For the moment, however, let's assume the validity of

the posttrib distinction between the wrath of God (at the end of the Tribulation) and other forms of wrath, judgment, and tribulation (throughout). Will the wrath of God be confined to the end only?

To answer yes, as the posttribulationist must, then two verses will have to be interpreted in specific ways. Revelation 6:17 must be understood to mean that God's wrath (absent from the earth up to that point) is about to break forth. Usually the word indicates that God's wrath has previously been poured out in the preceding judgments and continues to be poured out under the sixth seal judgment. In other words, the more normal interpretation says that the wrath of God will not begin with the sixth seal but will start with the preceding judgments. And, of course, the preceding judgments will have occurred earlier in the Tribulation period, for they cannot all be bunched at the end.

Revelation 15:1 states that the last series of plagues (the bowl judgments) finish, or complete, the wrath (literally, anger) of God on the earth. No one debates that the seven bowl judgments must come to pass before God's anger can be finished. The question is not, When will God's anger be finished? The question is, When will it begin? If something is going to be finished when certain events occur, then by all the principles of normal understanding, something must have begun before those events. The seven bowl judgments complete God's wrath; therefore, the wrath of God does not begin with those judgments. It has to begin before. The wrath of God will be finishing, not beginning, at the time of the seven bowl judgments.

But the posttributionist must have God's wrath begin at the end of the Tribulation; otherwise, the church will not escape, since the rapture will be the means of escape and does not come until the end. So the rapture and the wrath of God have to be at the end, and God's wrath cannot begin before then (though other kinds of trouble can). But does not Revelation 15:1 negate the claim that God's anger will be limited to the very end of the Tribulation? It must begin some time previous to the pouring out of these last judgments. And any time is too much time for a posttrib rapture that is a single event with the second coming.

Gundry thinks that the pretrib interpretation of Revelation 15:1 "overloads" the meaning of *finish* or *complete*.[2] Judge for yourself whether it is an overload or a normal understanding.

Protection and/or Removal?

Posttributionists believe the church will survive the Tribulation because it will be protected, but more specifically protected from divine wrath yet still subject to the wrath of Satan, Antichrist, and men. Actually, the posttrib position is both protection and removal: protection during the entire Tribulation (in case God's wrath falls before the finale of the Tribulation[3]), and removal at the end in the rapture.

Posttribulationists acknowledge that there will be martyrs during the Tribulation, so not all the redeemed will be protected. Actually, then, it will be a selective protection, not a universal one. But on what basis will God protect some and allow others to die? Apparently on a more accidental basis than on a divinely ordered one. Geography seems to be a factor, for it is suggested that those in and near Israel will more likely be martyred. But those who escape and survive will be raptured at the end. Everything considered, a decimated church will be given survival protection to live on until the rapture.

Often this selective protection is likened to the protection Israel experienced when the plagues fell on the Egyptians. Now, of course God can protect and preserve anyone's life anytime and anywhere He chooses. Israel was protected from the plagues that troubled Egypt because the Israelites lived apart in the land of Goshen. Saints during the Tribulation will live throughout the world, making it difficult to see how they will be able to escape the effects of the destruction of vegetation (Revelation 8:7-8), or the death of creatures in the seas (Revelation 8:9), or the embittering of rivers and springs (Revelation 8:10-11).

So the posttrib answer about the church is that some will be martyred, some will be protected, and survivors will be raptured. The protection is partial, and the rapture of survivors is total. In other words, in the Tribulation, the church will experience both wrath (at least the wrath of

Satan and man, which will kill some) and rapture (of all who survive to the end).

The Promise of Revelation 3:10

"Because you have kept the word of My perseverance, I also will keep you from the hour of testing, that hour which is about to come upon the whole world, to test those who dwell upon the earth" (Revelation 3:10). That this promise concerns the church's relation to the Tribulation period is almost never debated (posttrib Douglas Moo acknowledges this as well[4]). The reason is in the verse itself. This time of trial "is about to come on all the inhabited earth." It is worldwide, and on this inhabited earth— that is, on its people. It had not happened up to that time, for it was still in the future—"about to come." It is not a promise restricted to the church at Philadelphia in the first century any more than favorite promises like Philippians 4:13 or 4:19 or 1 Corinthians 10:13 were limited to the churches in the first century. Also, the risen Lord said in all seven letters in Revelation 2 and 3 that all the churches should heed what He said.

Posttribulationists have difficulty interpreting this promise in a straightforward way. One says that it "need not be a promise of a removal from the very physical presence of tribulation. It is a promise of preservation and deliverance in and through it."[5] More particularly, the phrase "I will keep you from the hour" (*tereso ek tes horas*) is dissected in order to support a posttrib rapture after preservation through the Tribulation. "From" (*ek*) is assigned the meaning "out from within," or "emergence," to indicate that the church will be in the Tribulation and then emerge from it at the end. "I will keep" (*tereso*) is understood as "I will guard," again indicating that the church will be protected on earth throughout the Tribulation. Thus the posttributionist understands the promise to mean that the church will be guarded through the seven years of Tribulation and then emerge from it at the close in the posttrib rapture/second coming.

But remember, the protection will be partial and selective at best. From the wrath of Satan and Antichrist alone, many saints will die during the Tribulation and will *in no way* experience the promise of Revelation 3:10 if the worldwide time of testing refers to the entire Tribulation period. Some posttributionists, however, assign the hour of testing only to the very last Tribulation crisis, and they understand the promise to mean that the church will be raptured just before the last judgments, and thus protected by removal.

But here, the posttrib position is being inconsistent. If the promise means to guard throughout the entire period, then it is a promise only selectively and partially fulfilled. If the promise relates only to the last crisis, then the church is *not* promised protection during almost all the seven years prior to that last crisis. The promise then relates only to the rapture at the end of the Tribulation. This understanding is more in accord with the posttrib interpretation of the beginning of the Day of the Lord. But that interpretation understands the promise to mean the same thing as the pretribulationist says it means: deliverance by rapture, not deliverance by protection. The only difference is that we disagree on when that deliverance will take place. If it takes place at the beginning of the seven years, the deliverance is by removal from the earth; if near or at the end, then the deliverance is by supernatural protection while the church is on the earth during the Tribulation until the rapture at the end.

Posttribulationists say that "from" (*ek*) refers to the church's protection within the Tribulation. Pretribulationists understand it to mean preservation by being absent from the Tribulation. One is an internal protection (living through the Tribulation); the other is an external protection (being in heaven during that time). Which meaning does "from" (*ek*) support?

If the preposition is considered alone, the answer is either. But, for the record, *ek* does denote a position outside something without implying a prior position inside and then emergence from within.

The pretrib understanding of *ek* is supported by a number of verses that have nothing to do with the rapture and therefore do not beg the question. Proverbs 21:23 says, "He who guards his mouth and his tongue guards his soul from troubles." Guarding your mouth and tongue is not the means of protecting yourself in the time of trouble; rather, it is the means of escaping potential trouble. In the Septuagint translation, the *ek* indicates an external, not internal, preservation. *Ek* is also used in the same way of external protection in Joshua 2:13 and in Psalms 33:19; 56:13.

Likewise, in the New Testament, *ek* clearly has the same meaning. In Acts 15:29, Gentile believers were asked to keep themselves *from* certain practices that were offensive to Jewish believers. The only way they could do that would be by abstaining entirely from the practices. They must withdraw from the activities they were practicing, not somehow protect themselves while continuing to practice those things. According to James 5:20, if a sinning Christian can be turned away from his backslidden state, he will be saved *from* physical death. There is no way *ek* could mean he will be protected in the midst of physical death and then emerge from it in some kind of resurrection. He will escape a premature death by being exempt from it.[6]

Posttribs attempt to invalidate the force of these examples by insisting that since they do not relate to spatial removal (moving from one space to another), they cannot be used to understand Revelation 3:10 as spatial removal from earth to heaven. But that imposes a meaning on *ek* that is not a necessary part of its meaning. To be removed from trouble means you do not experience that trouble anymore (Proverbs 21:23). To abstain from offending practices means you do not do them anymore (Acts 15:29). To be kept from the hour of trial means you are not in that time of trouble, and since it will come upon all the people of the earth, how can you be kept from it unless you are removed from this earth? And that means a pretrib rapture.

The same phrase, *keep from,* occurs in John 17:15: "I do not ask Thee to take them out of the world, but to keep them from the evil one." Posttribulationists point out that this promise is fulfilled not by removing believers from the world but by protecting them from Satan while they live on the earth. Then they assert that, similarly, believers will live during the Tribulation but be kept from its wrath.

Such an analogy fails to answer the basic question, How are believers kept from Satan's power? True, it is not by removing them from this world, but a removal is involved. Paul described it this way: "He delivered us from the domain of darkness, and transferred us to the kingdom of His beloved Son" (Colossians 1:13). John said the same thing when he wrote that "the evil one does not touch [cling to] him [the believer]" (1 John 5:18). Believers have been transferred from one domain (Satan's) to another (Christ's), and that is how we are kept from the evil one.

However, the promise of Revelation 3:10 not only guarantees being kept from Tribulation trials but from the Tribulation period itself. The promise is not, "I will keep you from the trials." It is, "I will keep you from the *hour* of the trials." Posttribulationists find means to "undercut stress on the term 'hour'"[7] by insisting that "hour" means the experience of a time period but not the time itself. In other words, the church will live through the time but not experience (some of) the events. But if the events of the Tribulation are worldwide, and directly and indirectly affect everybody, how can the church be on the earth and escape the experiences? If our Lord had been saved from the hour of His atoning sacrifice (John 12:27) by living through that time but by not experiencing the events of His passion, there would have been no atonement.

If, as posttribs say, the promise is that the church will live through the Tribulation under divine protection and emerge at the end, then why was a different preposition not used that would clearly convey that meaning? For instance, "in" (*en*) would mean that the church would be kept (safely) in that time. Or why not "through" (*dia*), which would mean kept through the Tribulation? Why "from" (*ek*)? Because that means the church will be removed from the time, and that means a pretrib rapture.

Granted, it is possible to live through a time and miss some of the events (like being present at an amusement park but missing some of the rides). But it is not possible to miss the time without also missing the events.

To summarize, posttribulationists teach unclearly the meaning of the promise of Revelation 3:10: 1) For some, it means protection (for some believers who escape martyrdom throughout the Tribulation) and then rapture at the end. 2) For some, it means protection from the last crisis (which includes Armageddon and the "lull" of peace and safety that supposedly precedes it) by rapture just before that last crisis. 3) For others, it means the church will live through Armageddon, be guarded during that time, and emerge (all believers unscathed?) in the rapture/second coming. One thing is clear to posttribulationists: It cannot mean deliverance before the Tribulation begins.

Yet the promise is clear and plain: "I...will keep you from the hour of testing." Not from just any persecution, but from the coming time that will affect the whole earth. (The only way to escape worldwide trouble is not to be on the earth.) And the church is to be kept not from just the events but from the time. And the only way to escape the time when events take place is not to be in a place where time ticks on. The only place that meets those qualifications is heaven.

Perhaps an illustration will help. As a teacher, I frequently give exams. Let's suppose that I announce an exam will occur on such and such a day at the regular class time. Then suppose I say, "I want to make a promise to students whose grade average for the semester so far is *A*. The promise is: I will keep you from the exam."

Now, I could keep my promise to those *A* students this way: I could tell them to come to the exam, pass out the exam to everyone, and give to the *A* students a sheet containing the answers. They would take the exam and yet in reality be kept from the exam. They would live through the time but not suffer the trial. This is posttribulationism: protection while enduring.

But if I said to the class, "I am giving an exam next week. I want to make a promise to all the *A* students. I will keep you from the hour of the exam." They would understand clearly that to be kept from the hour of the test exempts them from being present during that hour. This is pretribulationism, and this is the meaning of the promise of Revelation 3:10. And the promise came from the risen Savior who Himself is the deliverer from the wrath to come (1 Thessalonians 1:10).

The rapture is the hope of the church. To be sure, it is the hope of pretribs, midtribs, and posttribs. If our Lord had planned that we endure part or all of the Tribulation, we would accept that as His will. If He promised to remove us from that awful time, we should thank Him most gratefully. But whatever view we hold, we know that when He appears, we will be like Him—pure, without sin, and righteous (1 John 3:2-7). Therefore, every day until we die or are raptured, we should continually be purifying our lives (1 John 3:3), be abounding in the work of the Lord (1 Corinthians 15:58), and be loving His appearing (2 Timothy 4:8).

He says, "I am coming quickly." We say, "Come, Lord Jesus" (Revelation 22:20).

NOTES

Chapter 2—Are the Questions Important?

1. Douglas J. Moo, "The Case for the Posttribulation Rapture Position," *The Rapture: Pre-, Mid-, or Post-Tribulational?* (Grand Rapids, MI: Zondervan, 1984), 208.

2. Renald Showers, *Maranatha Our Lord, Come!* (Ballmawr, NJ: The Friends of Israel Gospel Ministry, 1995), 127-28.

Chapter 5—The Vocabulary for the Second Coming

1. George E. Ladd, *The Blessed Hope* (Grand Rapids, MI: Eerdmans, 1956), 69. This same argument continues to be used by Douglas Moo, "Posttribulation Rapture," *The Rapture: Pre-, Mid-, or Post-Tribulational?* (Grand Rapids, MI: Zondervan, 1984), 176-78.

2. Robert H. Gundry, *The Church and the Tribulation* (Grand Rapids, MI: Zondervan, 1973), 162.

3. Ladd, *The Blessed Hope*, 70.

Chapter 6—What Does 2 Thessalonians 1 Really Say?

1. Robert H. Gundry, *The Church and the Tribulation* (Grand Rapids, MI: Zondervan, 1973), 113.

Chapter 7—Where Is the Church in Revelation 4–18?

1. George E. Ladd, *The Blessed Hope* (Grand Rapids, MI: Eerdmans, 1956), 165.

2. Douglas J. Moo, "The Case for the Posttribulation Rapture Position," *The Rapture: Pre-, Mid-, or Post-Tribulational?* (Grand Rapids, MI: Zondervan, 1984), 201.

Chapter 8—Where Did the Pretrib View Originate?

1. George E. Ladd, *The Blessed Hope* (Grand Rapids, MI: Eerdmans, 1956), 43-54.

2. R.A. Huebner, *The Truth of the Pre-Tribulation Rapture Recovered* (Morganville, NJ: Present Truth Publishers, n.d.), 21-25.

3. Ernest R. Sandeen, *The Roots of Fundamentalism* (Chicago, IL: University of Chicago Press, 1970), 64.

4. Dave MacPherson, *The Incredible Cover-Up* (Plainfield, NJ: Logos International, 1975), especially 31-32.

5. Ibid., 85.

6. Ibid., 151-54.

7. Ibid., 154-55.

8. Ibid., 143.

9. Sandeen, *Roots of Fundamentalism,* 34; and Huebner, *Truth of the Pre-Tribulation Rapture,* 74.

10. James Orr, *The Progress of Dogma* (Grand Rapids, MI: Eerdmans, 1952), 24-30.

Chapter 9—Populating the Millennial Kingdom

1. Robert H. Gundry, *The Church and the Tribulation* (Grand Rapids, MI: Zondervan, 1973), 81-83, 134-39, 163-71.

2. Ibid., 83.

3. Ibid., 137.

4. Ibid.

5. George E. Ladd, *A Commentary on the Revelation of John* (Grand Rapids, MI: Eerdmans, 1972), 114.

6. Gundry, *The Church and the Tribulation,* 168.

7. Ibid., 166.

8. Ibid., 137.

9. Ibid., 167.

Chapter 10—The Day of the Lord

1. Robert H. Gundry, *The Church and the Tribulation* (Grand Rapids, MI: Zondervan, 1973), 77.

2. Ibid., 48.

3. Ibid., 76.

4. Henry Alford, *The Greek New Testament*, 4 vols. (London: Rivingtons, 1875), 4:622.

5. Ibid., 4:665.

6. Marvin Rosenthal, *The Pre-Wrath Rapture of the Church* (Nashville, TN: Nelson, 1990), 117.

7. Gundry, *The Church and the Tribulation*, 92.

8. Ibid., 95.

9. Ibid., 77.

10. Ibid., 92.

11. Ibid.

12. Douglas J. Moo, "The Case for the Posttribulation Rapture Position," *The Rapture: Pre-, Mid-, or Post-Tribulational?* (Grand Rapids, MI: Zondervan, 1984), 182-83. Moo, though a New Testament scholar, overlooks Paul's use of *peri de* here.

Chapter 11—Wrath or Rapture?

1. Robert H. Gundry, *The Church and the Tribulation* (Grand Rapids, MI: Zondervan, 1973), 49.

2. Ibid., 48.

3. Ibid., 47.

4. Douglas J. Moo, "The Case for the Posttribulation Rapture Position," *The Rapture: Pre-, Mid-, or Post-Tribulational?* (Grand Rapids, MI: Zondervan, 1984), 197.

5. George E. Ladd, *The Blessed Hope* (Grand Rapids, MI: Eerdmans, 1956), 85-86.

6. For an excellent discussion of these and other points related to Revelation 3:10, see Jeffrey L. Townsend, "The Rapture in Revelation 3:10," *Bibliotheca Sacra,* July 1980, 252-66.

7. Gundry, *The Church and the Tribulation* (Grand Rapids, MI: Zondervan, 1973), 59.

To learn more about our
Harvest Prophecy resources, please visit:

www.HarvestProphecyHQ.com

HARVEST PROPHECY
<small>An Imprint of Harvest House Publishers</small>